The Fort Cemetery
at Hierakonpolis

Studies in Egyptology

Edited by W. V. Davies, Deputy Keeper,
    Department of Egyptian Antiquities,
    The British Museum.

Editorial Adviser: A. F. Shore, Professor of Egyptology,
    University of Liverpool.

The Fort Cemetery
at Hierakonpolis

(Excavated by John Garstang)

Barbara Adams

with a contribution by Michael A. Hoffmann

Routledge
Taylor & Francis Group

ﾉNDON AND NEW YORK

First published in 1987 by
Kegan Paul Limited

This edition first published in 2009 by
Routledge
2 Park Square, Milton Park, Abingdon, Oxon, OX14 4RN

Simultaneously published in the USA and Canada
by Routledge
52 Vanderbilt Avenue, New York, NY 10017

First issued in paperback 2013

Routledge is an imprint of the Taylor & Francis Group, an informa business

British Library Cataloguing in Publication Data
A catalogue record for this book is available from the British Library

Publisher's Note
The publisher has gone to great lengths to ensure the quality of this reprint
but points out that some imperfections in the original copies may be
apparent. The publisher has made every effort to contact original copyright
holders and would welcome correspondence from those they have been
unable to trace.

ISBN 13: 978-0-4158-6526-5 (pbk)
ISBN 13: 978-0-7103-0275-5 (hbk)

CONTENTS

LIST OF PLATES

Plate 1   Grave 6 (H1) and Grave 8 (H3)

Plate 2   Grave 9 (H4, ... nd Grave 10 (H6)

Plate 3   Grave 11 (H8) and Grave 16 (H11)

Plate 4   Graves 19 & 20 (H16) and Grave 25 (H23)

Plate 5   Grave 26 (H24) and Grave 28 (H26)

Plate 6   Grave 29 (H28) and Grave 32 (H30)

Plate 7   Grave 35 (H33) and Grave 37 (H36)

Plate 8   Grave 42 (H37) and Grave 43 (H38)

Plate 9   Grave 47 (H38) and Grave 50 (H42)

Plate 10   Grave 52 (H45) and Grave 53 (H44)

Plate 11   Grave 56 (H86) and Grave 60 (H46)

Plate 12   Grave 61 (H49) and Grave 62 (H47)

Plate 13   Grave 66 (H96) and Grave 68 (H51)

Plate 14   Grave 70 (H54) and Grave 71 (H55)

Plate 15   Grave 74 (H58) and Grave 76 (H59)

Plate 16   Grave 81 (H61) and Grave 88 (H64)

Plate 17   Graves 88 & 89 (H65) and Grave 90 (H66)

Plate 18   Grave 92 (H69) and Grave 93 (H70)

PREFACE AND ACKNOWLEDGEMENTS

My involvement with the site of Hierakonpolis and its
excavators goes back to the early 1970s when, through
the inspiration and encouragement of Professor H. S.
Smith, the Head of the Egyptology Department at
University College London, I began work on the material
excavated there by J. E. Quibell and F. W. Green in
1898-1900. This fuller treatment of their results was
published in 1974 as *Ancient Hierakonpolis* and *Supplement*. By that time I was aware that Hierakonpolis was
being investigated again by the Americans, led by
Professor Walter A. Fairservis of Vassar College,
Poughkeepsie, New York, who undertook his first expedition to work in the town site in 1969. There he had
with him an Anthropology student called Michael Allen
Hoffman, who also began work in the Predynastic sites
in the desert. In 1978, Dr. Hoffman returned with his
own archaeological team to continue work in the
Predynastic areas; whilst the excavation of the town
and temple site (Kom el Gemuwia) was continued by
Professor Fairservis. Hoffman and his team returned to
Egypt in 1979 and he asked me to join the expedition in
the early part of 1980. I have been a member of the
Hierakonpolis research team ever since, having returned
to the site in 1981 (with Fairservis), 1982, 1984 and
1986 (with Hoffman).

Here I can take the opportunity to record my deep
appreciation to both leaders of the American expedition
for involving me in their work and giving me the
opportunity to gain far more of a sense of the site than
the immersion in publications, objects and old notebooks
had hitherto given me. I can only hope that my particular abilities have and will contribute to the aims of
the important research that the investigations of
Hierakonpolis represent.

It was at Hierakonpolis in 1980 that Dr. Hoffman
commented that the work of all previous excavators ought
to be fully covered as a complement to the results of the
present excavations. He was prompted by a visit from
Thomas Logan, then of the Metropolitan Museum, New York,
who was working on the material excavated by Ambrose
Lansing in 1934 (Lansing, 1935) in the continuation of
the Predynastic cemetery south of the Fort (Locality
Hk-27) on behalf of that museum. I had already covered
the first excavation by Quibell and Green and this left
the gap between them when Garstang was at the site in
1905-6 and de Morgan in 1907-8. (Winifred Needler has
now published Henri de Morgan's excavations, see Needler,
1984.) I agreed to explore the remaining British
possibilities and to write a summary of Garstang's
excavations.

On my return to England, I visited the School of
Archaeology and Oriental Studies at Liverpool University
where I knew that Garstang's records were deposited.
Professor A. F. Shore, the Head of Department, generously
assigned the relevant manuscripts, photographs and
material to me. During that visit it was obvious that
more could be produced than a brief summary of Garstang's
excavations at Hierakonpolis. This has in fact already
been admirably done for the Fort and the cemetery
beneath it in a preliminary paper by Barry Kemp (1963),
a former student at Liverpool.

For this publication I decided to concentrate on the
cemetery excavated within the mud brick Fort at the
opening of the Great Wadi and to follow Kemp's trail
which involved contacting the museums to which Garstang
sent objects in the hope that I could obtain a fuller
record of the material. The likely distribution was
extensive, as noted in a report to the Liverpool
excavation committee in 1905 (see Appendix A2), where
Garstang says he intended to make up sets of pots and
send them to museums in such places as Jamaica, South
Africa and Australia, as well as others in Canada, New
Zealand and the U.S.A. In fact I received a very
reasonable response to my queries about the material as
some curators have discovered more objects in their
museums since the 1960s. It is not at all unusual that
the original site numbers on the Egyptian material they
received from Garstang's excavations may have been lost
(see Chapter 1, footnote 2), but all in all, I think I
have succeeded in tracking down the maximum number of
objects. The personal help I received, together with
that gained from correspondence, has produced a
formidable list of curators and others I wish to acknow-
ledge here.

In some cases, such as Milwaukee, the supposed objects never turned up, and in Jamaica an earthquake removed them; from other places I never received replies, but the following people gave positive and negative replies to my queries about objects with an F number on them; Mrs. Angela P. Thomas, Bolton Museum and Art Gallery; Mr. A. M. Llewellyn, Blackburn Museum; Mr. Philip H. Watson, Birmingham Museum; Mrs. Margaret Warhurst and Mr. Edmund Southworth, National Museums and Galleries on Merseyside (ex. Merseyside County Museum), Liverpool; Dr. Jeffrey Spencer, British Museum; Dr. Oliver Watson and Mr. D. M. Archer, Victoria and Albert Museum, London; Mr. George B. Deakin; Ms. Pauline Beswick, Sheffield Museum; Mr. T. M. Ambrose, Lincoln Museum; Mrs. K. B. Griffiths, Wellcome Museum, Swansea University, Wales; Mr. C. J. Delaney, Carmarthen Museum, Wales; Mr. Charles Hunt, Anthropolog-ical Museum, University of Aberdeen, Scotland; Dr. L. F. Keppie, Hunterian Museum, Glasgow, Scotland; Dr. Nicholas Millet, Royal Ontario Museum, Toronto, Canada; Miss C. A. Lawler, Nicholson Museum, Sydney, Australia; Ms. Zoe Wakelin-King, Australian Museum, Sydney; Ms. Moya Smith, Western Australian Museum, Sydney; Ms. Joan Beck, Macquarie University, New South Wales, Australia; Dr. D. J. Robinson, Queensland Museum, Australia; Ms. Helen Reeves, Grainger Museum, University of Melbourne, Australia; Dr. Jill Hamel, Otago Museum, New Zealand; Mr. Carter Lupton, Milwaukee Museum, Wisconsin, U.S.A.; Mr. John A. Aarons, National Library of Jamaica, and last, but not least, Miss Patricia Winker, Professor Shore's secretary who also curates the teaching collection at the School of Archaeology and Oriental Studies, Liverpool University, for all her attention and the objects she kept finding for me to identify.

Theya Molleson, a past colleague from the Sub-Department of Anthropology at the British Museum of Natural History, kindly perused all the photographs of the graves in order to see if any of the bodies could be sexed or aged. Professor Fekri A. Hassan, of Washington State University, U.S.A., checked and criticised the cemetery analysis and regional perspective, and provided useful information about comparable data from Naqada; this scholarly contribution is deeply appreciated.

Dr. Stuart Munro Hay re-drew the plan of the Fort cemetery from Barry Kemp's original and added the newly plotted graves and shading. Barry Kemp relinquished his prior claim to the Garstang Hierakonpolis manuscripts so that I could make full use of them here. Anne Oxenham of the Geography Department, University College London, prepared several dyelines of the completed map for my various colleagues.

Mrs. Joan Crowfoot Payne, ex-Ashmolean Museum, Oxford,

helped greatly with the compilation of the Addenda and Corrigenda to the *Supplement* of *Ancient Hierakonpolis*, and Miss Caroline Ellis thoughtfully drew my attention to the objects in Maidstone Museum from Green's excavations.

Professor H. S. Smith has encouraged my continued interest in Hierakonpolis in recent years and has contributed U.C.L. Egyptology departmental funds to the production of this publication.

In addition to the facilities made available to me by the School of Archaeology and Oriental Studies in Liverpool, and the hospitality always afforded me there, Professor Shore provided the photographs of the graves through his department, together with permission to reproduce them here, for which he is owed a further debt of gratitude. He has read the text and made various valuable suggestions, but any errors which remain are my sole responsibility.

Various financial complications prevented this work from becoming a second Predynastic monograph through the Hierakonpolis expedition but, through a fortuitous meeting with W. V. Davies, Deputy Keeper of Egyptian Antiquities at the British Museum and Editor of the Kegan Paul International Studies in Egyptology series, this publication was finally made possible. The gratitude of the Hierakonpolis expedition is therefore due to him and Peter Hopkins of KPI for seeing it through to completion. Mrs. Elizabeth Keyzar, of the Department of Egyptology, U.C.L., patiently and painstakingly produced the camera-ready text, as always alert for omissions on my part, functioning as much more than a typist.

I hope that this presentation of the major part of Garstang's excavation at Hierakonpolis will contribute to the publication of his work, which was ably begun by Dorothy Downes on Esna in 1974 and is now being continued by other scholars.

Barbara Adams
Petrie Museum of Egyptian Archaeology,
University College London.

November, 1986.

In 1905, John Garstang held a concession to dig at
Hierakonpolis on behalf of the Liverpool University
Excavations Committee. He published a brief report
(Garstang, 1907) which described further excavations
within the temple and town enclosure of Nekhen, following those of Quibell and Green (1900 and 1902). During
his first season the ground had been too hard to
continue work in the town site, so he turned his
attention to the area of the mud brick "Fort" (on the
north side of the entrance to the Great Wadi, or Abul
Suffian, map in Quibell and Green, 1902, pls. LXXIIA,
LXXIV and Hoffman, *et al*, 1982, endpiece). Within the
Fort he excavated a Predynastic cemetery of some 188
graves, but only illustrated and mentioned a few of the
artifacts from them in his preliminary report. In the
second season at the site, Harold Jones continued the
trench in the temple area at the town site of Nekhen,
finding, among other objects, the head of the lapis
lazuli figure (Ash.E1057) which had been discovered by
Quibell in 1898, and Garstang went further south to dig
and survey. There are unpublished miscellaneous objects
from the work of Garstang and Jones at Nekhen in Liverpool, in both the University and Merseyside collections
(1), the most notable being an ivory tube in the latter
museum with the incised depiction of an early shrine,
published by a former Keeper (Slow, 1963-4). This
present work concentrates on the objects from the Predynastic cemetery beneath the Fort.

It is a great pity that Garstang left so many of his
excavations in Egypt unpublished because, judging by the
Hierakonpolis notebooks in Liverpool University, he was
a thorough worker who meticulously plotted and recorded
virtually every grave (166 of the 188), and photographed
many of them. In this respect his work compares favourably with that of Green, whose notebooks on the Hiera-

konpolis excavations of 1898-9 I analysed and published
(Adams, 1974b) and certainly with the notebooks that
Petrie kept in Egypt (Adams, 1975; Drower, 1985). The
situation was partially remedied by Barry Kemp (Kemp,
1963), who described the architecture of the Fort and
reconstructed a map of the cemetery using the sketch
plans among the manuscripts and the plotting measurements in the dig notebooks. I have decided to extend
his work and present the records from the notebooks i)
and ii) in full with a selection of photographs, so that
the full history of British archaeological work at
Hierakonpolis can be assembled. The American work at
the site by Lansing in 1934 will be presented by the
Metropolitan Museum, New York, to complete the earlier
reports and lead into those of the modern work there
since 1967 (Fairservis, 1971-2, 1983, 1986; Hoffman,
1971-2, 1974, 1980a,b, 1982, 1983, 1986; Lupton, 1980).
Winifred Needler has now completed and published the
Predynastic material in Brooklyn, which includes Henri
de Morgan's excavations at Hierakonpolis in 1907-8
(Needler, 1984).

The record here is a facsimile of the drawings and notes
in the notebooks laid out in a standard format for each
grave with the negative numbers of the Liverpool University archive added and the museum numbers of objects
where they are known. Obviously, the grave records are
not all consistent, due to the pace at which the work
progressed (the whole cemetery was dug between 16th
January and 11th February, 1905), but the majority have
orientation and individual sketches of the objects.
Sometimes there were extra notes on details such as the
condition of the bones and the remaining hair, but there
was virtually no sexing or ageing of the bodies, and
little can be deduced from the photographs, but males,
females and juveniles were present. What has proved
possible is the typing of the pottery from Garstang's
drawings and photographs and, more certainly, those I
have been able to locate in museums (2), using the
corpuses published by Petrie (Petrie, 1921, 1953). I
have then been able to assign Sequence Dates to the
graves and the Stufen (stages) of Kaiser (Kaiser, 1957).
Kemp had begun this process by using the pottery in the
Liverpool University collection. The convention I have
followed is as follows: S.D.31-39 to Naqada ·I, S.D.40-
62 to Naqada II, S.D.63-76 to Naqada III, and S.D.77-81
to the First Dynasty(3). Kemp's conclusion that the
cemetery ranges in date only from the Gerzean (Naqada II)
period to the transition from Predynastic to Early
Dynastic times, with the majority of the graves at
Stufen IIIa2-IIIb, is confirmed.

The following section is an attempt by myself and
Michael Hoffman to analyse and comment on the results

of the 1905 excavation in the Fort, and to fit them into
the wider context of the work at the site and elsewhere
in recent years. A model of what the coverage of a
Predynastic cemetery should be is provided by Dows
Dunham's publication of Lythgoe's excavation of the 7000
cemetery at Nag-ed-Dêr (Lythgoe, 1965). Unfortunately,
neither the information which can be gleaned from
Garstang's notebooks, nor the worldwide distribution of
the remaining objects, have permitted me to produce any-
thing emulating that tome within the economic stringen-
cies of these times. Rather, it is hoped that immediate
publication of this long-lost material in preference to
a future ideal production, unattainable at present, will
be understood and appreciated.

The Appendices cover the manuscripts and photographs in
Liverpool University, and present the distribution lists
of objects from the cemetery excavation which I have
been able to compile. Liverpool remains the main
location of the objects from Garstang's work, as well as
the repository of his records, and, since I began this
project, a number of extra objects have been located in
the stores of the University collection, identified and
added to the list. I do not doubt that others will turn
up, both there and in other institutions, but, as I
stated in the introduction to the *Supplement* on Green's
work at Hierakonpolis (Adams, 1974b), this work is also
meant as an aid to the future identification of objects
by museum curators(4), and the author will be pleased to
hear of any further rediscoveries that are made. As
travels to the U.S.A. and the passing years have proved
my premonition about the objects from the work of Quibell
and Green to be correct, I have also taken this opportunity to present the Addenda and Corrigenda to *Ancient
Hierakonpolis* and *Supplement* here as Appendix D.

The plates present the best selection of the photographs
of the graves taken in 1905, and the two samples of
Garstang's notebook entries (pl.25). A complete list of
the negatives in Liverpool, which also cover the Town and
Temple site of Nekhen, is included in Appendix B. I make
no apology for the inclusion of what may seem like
repetitious photographs of similar graves as a complement
to the grave records, as I know from experience that this
is what is needed by the student of the burial customs of
the Predynastic period. Too often the objects from a
grave may be located in a museum collection, but no
record of their original disposition in the grave was
published, as for instance in the case of the large
Predynastic cemeteries at Naqada and Ballas excavated by
Petrie and Quibell in 1895 (Petrie and Quibell, 1896;
Baumgartel, 1970). For records of these graves, recourse
may be made to the excavation notebooks in the Petrie
Museum at University College London where sketches of

many, but not all, of the graves may be found (notebooks listed in Adams, 1975; additional notebooks listed in Bourriau, 1984). The information from the additional notebooks was never included in the Supplement to the Naqada excavation (Baumgartel, 1970), and therefore has not been widely available to scholars. This situation is now rectified by the production of microfiche copies of all the Petrie *et al.* manuscript notebooks and tomb cards, which are also detailed year by year in Petrie's biography (Drower, 1985).

The map produced by Kemp has been re-drawn with the addition of a few graves, and the dates obtained from the analysis of the grave records have been indicated by shading to show the geographical distribution of the use of the cemetery. In 1978 and 1981, Professor Fairservis undertook further test excavations in the Fort and discovered some more Protodynastic graves near the north-west wall. The six graves he found at the higher level in the loose fill in 1978 may have been previously disturbed by Garstang; the bones were bunched and only one grave contained a coarse vessel. The line of his 1978 trench, which uncovered seven graves, is marked on this map. His intact grave 6, which contained twenty-one pottery vessels, corresponds to the overall Naqada III date of this part of the cemetery (unpublished information courtesy of Professor Fairservis).

For the abbreviations used in the following grave records, see Appendix C.

1.   These will be the subject of a separate paper.

2.   The marking method used on objects from the Fort
      cemetery was black ink and gives the grave number
      usually with "F" as a prefix or suffix, e.g. 19F or
      F19. Within the graves the objects were often given
      sub-letters, and these are sometimes marked on the
      object, e.g. F19b. Pots not assigned to a grave were
      were marked "F". Other localities at the site were
      designated as follows: "T" = the town site of Nekhen,
      "P" = palace, the temple area called the citadel by
      Quibell and Green. Therefore the objects from Hiera-
      konpolis can be distinguished from those excavated
      at other sites, e.g. "E" for Esna.

3.   There is now considerable debate (Kaiser and Dreyer,
      1982; Needler, 1984) about the acceptance of Narmer
      as the first king of the First Dynasty upon which
      this convention is based; therefore the Stufen III
      and Dynasty I groups here should be regarded as
      transitional and overlapping to allow for Narmer as
      a Protodynastic (or "Dynasty 0") ruler of Upper
      Egypt, and Hor-Aha as the first king of a united
      Egypt.

.   See note 2.

GRAVE RECORDS

based on Garstang notebooks i) and ii)
(see Appendix A)

Grave Number	Position in Cemetery	Date Excavated	Photograph Number
6	2.25 × 3.10	16th and 18th Jan. 1905	H.1

Sketch of Grave	Measurements	Bodies
	L: .80 m	One

Measurements		Sex
W: .80 m		Child

	Disturbed
Special Notes	No

Special Notes	Position
Body very broken	Head north
Four shells under arms	Face east

S.D.? 43-74

Stufen
? II d 2
Late Gerzean

Pottery

Drawing	Type	Museum Number	Other Objects Description	Museum Number
a	? R76G		3 flints in b	
b	?R26b or R33b	L.M.25.19.05.29 missing		
	? R67			

HIERAKONPOLIS FORT.   GARSTANG EXCAVATION,1905.   GRAVE RECORD

Grave Number	Position in Cemetery	Date Excavated	Photograph Number
7	2.80 × 2.90	16th Jan. 1905	H.2

Sketch of Grave	Measurements	Bodies

small pot

Measurements

L: 1.50 m

W: .85 m

Bodies

One

Sex

?

Disturbed

No

Special Notes

About 40 cm below old desert surface (that on which lowest row of bricks is built on).

Body on left side

Position

Head north
Face east

S.D. ? 47-75

Stufen

? II d 2

Late Gerzean

Pottery			Other Objects	
Drawing	Type	Museum Number	Description	Museum Number
	? R76p			
	? R57a			

Grave Number	Position in Cemetery	Date Excavated	Photograph Number
8	6.50 x 6.50	16th Jan. 1905	H.3

Sketch of Grave	Measurements	Bodies
	L: 1.25 m W: .80 m	One

		Sex
		?

		Disturbed
		No

	Special Notes	Position
	Head covered with pottery. Body lying on left side	Head north Face east
		S.D. ? 73-79
		Stufen ? IIIa2 Protodynastic

Pottery

Drawing	Type	Museum Number
large jar a	? 81f proto.corpus	
small basin b	? L19p	L.M.13 12.05 7 missing another bowl ? L16b AMS.E15664
tall jars with wave pattern c	? W61	
d	? W61	
inside A small vase	? L43p	

Other Objects

Description	Museum Number
slate palette type 95h	

HIERAKONPOLIS FORT.   GARSTANG EXCAVATION,1905.   GRAVE RECORD

Grave Number	Position in Cemetery	Date Excavated	Photograph Number
9	7.45 × 7.45	16th Jan. 1905	H.4

Sketch of Grave		Measurements	Bodies
		L: 1.60 m W: .90 m 50 cm below desert level	One
			Sex
			? Male
			Disturbed
		Special Notes	No
			Position
			Head south Face west S.D.? 78-79
			Stufen
			? IIIb Protodynastic - Dynasty I

Pottery			Other Objects	
Drawing	Type	Museum Number	Description	Museum Number
a	? Proto 87M5		b. Slate palette with eyes	
c	Proto ?92A		type 86	

HIERAKONPOLIS FORT.   GARSTANG EXCAVATION, 1905.   GRAVE RECORD

Grave Number	Position in Cemetery	Date Excavated	Photograph Number
10	8.60 x 9.15	16th Jan. 1905	H.5, H.6

Sketch of Grave		Measurements	Bodies
 2 rows beads	↓	L: 1.85 m	One

			Sex
			? Male

		Special Notes	Disturbed
		Two rows of beads and bone pin at back of head. Stone beads on left wrist Burial lying on left side & bound round with reeds & plaited rope 50cm below surface	No

Position

Head south
Face west
S.D. ?46-77

Stufen
IId2-IIIa1
Late Gerzean

Pottery			Other Objects	
Drawing	Type	Museum Number	Description	Museum Number
Four large vases a d e f	R84d		Beneath head - Slate palette type 46	?? L.D.E 5951
: dish under head	? R24m		Dish under head contained flint 5 bone hair pins with case and bone comb - broken	
n d was small pot			green carnelian	
nder arms ish and small ise decorated ith red stripes				

Grave Number	Position in Cemetery	Date Excavated	Photograph Number
11	7.40 x 6.20	16th Jan. 1905	H.8

Sketch of Grave	Measurements	Bodies
		One

	Measurements	
	L: 1.50 m	
	W: 1.00 m	**Sex** ? Male
		Disturbed No
	Special Notes Burial lying on left side	**Position** Head south Face west S.D. 76-79
		Stufen IIa2-IIIb Protodynastic- Dynasty I

Pottery

Other Objects

Drawing	Type	Museum Number	Description	Museum Number
a	L36h			
b	R26a			
c imperfect shape with perforated closed mouth.	L53s			
d	L58c			
e	W61			

HIERAKONPOLIS FORT.   GARSTANG EXCAVATION, 1905.   GRAVE RECORD

Grave Number	Position in Cemetery	Date Excavated	Photograph Number
12	11.00 × 9.25 105 W. of N.	16th Jan. 1905	H.9

Sketch of Grave		Measurements	Bodies

	Measurements	Bodies
	L: 1.20 m W: .60 m	One
		Sex ?
		Disturbed No
	Special Notes Square slate palette, broken, found 150 cm south by west of burial lying on left side	**Position** Head S.E. Face S.W.
		S.D. ?78-80
		Stufen ? IIIb Protodynastic Dynasty I

Pottery

Drawing

a

b

Type	Museum Number
Proto. cf. 63b painted: five vertical wavy lines	L.U. E4330
? L19-20	

Other Objects

Description	Museum Number

Grave Number	Position in Cemetery	Date Excavated	Photograph Number
Find spot 13 – not a grave		16th Jan. 1905	

Sketch of Grave		Measurements	Bodies _None_
			Sex
			Disturbed
		Special Notes	
		Found near each other	Position
			S.D. ?
			Stufen ?

Pottery

Drawing	Type	Museum Number	Other Objects	
			Description	Museum Number
black topped pot clay cover	? B81H	?Cat. 75.774	large flint	

Grave Number	Position in Cemetery	Date Excavated	Photograph Number
14	5.00 × 5.00	18th Jan. 1905	H.10

Sketch of Grave		Measurements	Bodies
		L: 1.40 m W: .80 m	one
			Sex Old Adult
			Disturbed No
		Special Notes Burial on left side bones very broken	**Position** Head north Face east S.D. ? 46·77
			Stufen ? IId2 - IIIa1 Late Gerzean

Pottery

Drawing	Type	Museum Number	**Other Objects** Description	Museum Number
a	? L53r			
b	? R76h or R76m			
(e d e f)	R24m			
g irregular	R84d	Bolt.44.05.16		

HIERAKONPOLIS FORT.   GARSTANG EXCAVATION,1905. GRAVE RECORD

Grave Number	Position in Cemetery	Date Excavated	Photograph Number
15	1.00 × 2.30 (to head)	18th Jan. 1905	

Sketch of Grave	Measurements	Bodies
	L: 1.75 m W: .70m	One

Sketch of Grave

Measurements	**Bodies**
L: 1.75 m	One
W: .70m	**Sex** ?
	Disturbed No
Special Notes	**Position** Extended Head east
Lying on back	**S.D.**
	Stufen Dynastic

Pottery			Other Objects	
Drawing	Type	Museum Number large bowl Bla.NN.	Description	Museum Number

HIERAKONPOLIS FORT.   GARSTANG EXCAVATION,1905.   GRAVE RECORD

Grave Number	Position in Cemetery	Date Excavated	Photograph Number
16	10.75 × 11.50	18th Jan. 1905	H.11

Sketch of Grave		Measurements	Bodies
		L: 1.20 m W: 0.75 m	One

Measurements		Bodies
L: 1.20 m		One
W: 0.75 m		

	Sex
	? Female

	Disturbed
Special Notes	No
"Old boy" lying on left side	
	Position
Male by large bones	Head south Face west
	S.D.? 77-80
	Stufen
	IIIa2 - IIIb Protodynastic- Dynasty I.

Pottery

Drawing	Type	Museum Number
a — red pot decorated with dark stripes & wave pattern in relief	W62	
b — inverted as cover of a)	L12d	L.M. 30.86.3
— small dish	? L2a	

Other Objects

Description	Museum Number

HIERAKONPOLIS FORT.   GARSTANG EXCAVATION,1905.   GRAVE RECORD

Grave Number	Position in Cemetery	Date Excavated	Photograph Number
17	Tomb 10 to 17- 3.25 " 16 " 17-2.10	18th Jan. 1905	H.15

Sketch of Grave		Measurements	Bodies
		L: 1.15 m W: 0.75 m	One
			Sex ? Female
			Disturbed No
		Special Notes	Position Head south Face west S.D. ?77-80
			Stufen ?IIIa2 -IIIb Protodynastic- Dynasty I

Pottery			Other Objects	
Drawing	Type	Museum Number	Description	Museum Number
	W61			
	L53k			

Grave Number	Position in Cemetery	Date Excavated	Photograph Number
18	14.45 × 13.15	18th Jan. 1905	H.13, H.14

Sketch of Grave		Measurements	Bodies
		L: 1.25 m W: 1.60m	One

	Measurements	Bodies
		Sex ?
		Disturbed No
	Special Notes	Position Head West Face north
	Adult burial lying on side	S.D.? 77-82
		Stufen IIIa 2-IIIb Protodynastic - Dynasty I

Pottery

Drawing	Type	Museum Number	Other Objects Description	Museum Number
	W61 and W62	Cat.75.769	slate palette	LU.E5379
	L36n			
	R26a			
	Proto. 63e			

slate palette

dish

bricks

Grave Number	Position in Cemetery	Date Excavated	Photograph Number
19 and 20 cont.→	11.50 × 12.85	19th Jan. 1905	H.15, H.16, H.17

Sketch of Grave	Measurements	Bodies

Measurements	**Bodies**
L: 1.30 m	2
W: 1.50 m	**Sex** ? Male Child
	Disturbed No

dish upturned under vases

Special Notes
Child burial no. 20 with beads on head, bones broken. Tall pots fitted into one another points of upper row being in mouths of lower row. Probably adult female and child

Position Heads south Faces west

S.D. 77-80

Stufen IIIa2 – IIIb Protodynastic – Dynasty I

Pottery

Drawing	Type	Museum Number		Museum Number
o	L 53 k	fine pottery all others coarse		
p	Proto. 3a	large dish — LM. 30.86.6		
f + i	R 76 p	vase LM. 25.11.05.26 missing	h. j. k — Proto. 60n	
g	Proto. 57 N		l m n — Proto. 60k	

cont....

Grave Number	Position in Cemetery	Date Excavated	Photograph Number
19 and 20 continued			

Sketch of Grave		Measurements	Bodies
			Sex
			Disturbed
		Special Notes	
		no. 20 child burial	Position
			S.D.
			Stufen

Pottery

Other Objects

Drawing	Type	Museum Number	Description	Museum Number
a small pot with wavy handles unglazed	W42G		d slate palette chipped type 87L	LM.13.12.05.10
small pot fine glaze dark red	? P95b or Proto. 87H⁶		pieces of tusk	
c similar to b larger not so finely finished			white carnelian beads dark green light green	LM.25.11.05.52
small dish found above	Proto.2m			
e	? Proto.17g			
all pots numbered 19				

HIERAKONPOLIS FORT.   GARSTANG EXCAVATION,1905.   GRAVE RECORD

Grave Number	Position in Cemetery	Date Excavated	Photograph Number
21	from bone mark 2.50 × 1.10	19th Jan. 1905	H.18

Sketch of Grave	Measurements	Bodies
	L: 1.10 m W: .70 m	One

		Sex
		?

		Disturbed
	Special Notes	No
	Head almost upright Few perforated shells + flint found under head	Position Head north Face west
		S.D ?77-81
		Stufen ?IIIb Protodynastic - Dynasty I

Pottery

Drawing	Type	Museum Number	Other Objects	
			Description	Museum Number
a	Proto. ?90B			
b	Proto. ?2d			
c	Proto. ?2R			

Grave Number	Position in Cemetery	Date Excavated	Photograph Number
22	6.25 × 6.95	20th Jan. 1905	H.19

Sketch of Grave	Measurements	Bodies
	L: 1.0 m W: 0.70 m	One

		Sex
		Male

		Disturbed
	Special Notes	Yes
	Lying on left side arms under head bones very broken legs very doubled up, no pots.	Position Head south Face north/east
		S.D. ?
		Stufen ?

Pottery			Other Objects	
Drawing	Type	Museum Number	Description	Museum Number

Grave Number	Position in Cemetery	Date Excavated	Photograph Number
23	8.90 × 10.25	20th Jan. 1905	H.20

Sketch of Grave	Measurements	Bodies
	L: 1.10 m W: 8.90 m	Two

		Sex
		Two children

		Disturbed
	Special Notes	Yes
	Child burial on right. Only head remains of left burial, bones all broken. Buried facing one another	Position Heads south [Face east] S.D.? 43-77 Stufen ?IId1-IIIa1 Gerzean-Protodynastic

Pottery

Drawing	Type	Museum Number
a	? R67	
b	R26c	LU.E4227
c	R21d	
E small pot under d	shape D61k	
f fine glaze dark red	cf. P46b	
g	? R57c	

Other Objects

Description	Museum Number
On head of burial on left were beads of various descriptions: double copper beads, perforated shells, amounts of kohl wrapped in cloth	
d traces of green cf. type 54j	LM.25.11.05.39

Grave Number	Position in Cemetery	Date Excavated	Photograph Number
24	8.10 × 9.25	20th Jan. 1905	H21

Sketch of Grave	Measurements	Bodies
⚓	L: 1.45 m W: 1.00 m	One

Measurements
L: 1.45 m
W: 1.00 m

Special Notes

Bodies	One
Sex	?Female
Disturbed	No
Position	Head south Face west
S.D.	?47-74
Stufen	? IId2-IIIa1 Late Gerzean

Pottery

Drawing	Type	Museum Number	Other Objects — Description	Museum Number
a	?R76H		Serpentine beads under head ○	
b fine clay	L53p	LU.E4430		
c	?R67			
d + ε	R84D			

above

HIERAKONPOLIS FORT.   GARSTANG EXCAVATION,1905.   GRAVE RECORD

Grave Number	Position in Cemetery	Date Excavated	Photograph Number
25	10.40 × 11.45	20th Jan. 1905	H.23

Sketch of Grave	Measurements	Bodies
	L: 1.70 m W: 1.00 m	One

Measurements
L: 1.70 m
W: 1.00 m

Special Notes
Under grave 17

Bodies — One
Sex — Male
Disturbed — No
Position — Head south Face west
S.D. 46-78
Stufen IId1 - IId2 Late Gerzean

Pottery

Drawing	Type	Museum Number
d / a + c	R84h	
b	? P11b shape	
e + f (smaller than a) decorated with dark stripes handles in relief	W14 W43b	f. LM.16.11.06.139 missing E Burnley EG 241
h	? R24	
i	? L12D	

Other Objects

Description	Museum Number
g Slate palette traces of green	LU.E5306

HIERAKONPOLIS FORT.   GARSTANG EXCAVATION,1905.   GRAVE RECORD

Grave Number	Position in Cemetery	Date Excavated	Photograph Number
26	Under inner east wall of Fort		H.24

Sketch of Grave	Measurements	Bodies
	L: 1.55 m W: 0.40m	One
		Sex ? Female
		Disturbed No
	Special Notes	Position Extended Head west
	Lying on back under wall	S.D.
		Stufen Dynastic

Pottery			Other Objects	
Drawing	Type	Museum Number	Description	Museum Number

HIERAKONPOLIS FORT.   GARSTANG EXCAVATION,1905.   GRAVE RECORD

Grave Number	Position in Cemetery	Date Excavated	Photograph Number
27	10.00 x 7.00 to corner		H.25

Sketch of Grave		Measurements	Bodies One

	Sex
	Adolescent

Special Notes	Disturbed
Infant burial surrounded by coarse stones on all sides. To south are two large pots	No

Position
Head N-W

S.D 747-78

Stufen ? II d2
Late Gerzean

Pottery

Drawing	Type	Museum Number	Other Objects Description	Museum Number
Small vase good glaze	? P93b		2 flints	
pointed pot very coarse	?R76p			

Grave Number	Position in Cemetery	Date Excavated	Photograph Number
28	8.85 × 6.75 to south end	20th Jan. 1905	H.26

Sketch of Grave

Measurements

L: 1.25 m

W: 0.80 m

Special Notes

Lying on left side

Bodies

One

Sex ?

Disturbed No

Position

Head north
Face east

S.D. 52-76

Stufen IId2

Late Gerzean

Pottery

Drawing	Type	Museum Number	**Other Objects** Description	Museum Number
pot with two handles in wave form a	W43B	Bol. 44.05.34		
g h e	R84			
d partly under c .d,b,f	?R24a			

Grave Number	Position in Cemetery	Date Excavated	Photograph Number
29	Under wall	20th Jan. 1905	H.27 H.28

Sketch of Grave		Measurements	Bodies One
			Sex ?
			Disturbed Broken coffin
		Special Notes	
		Burial in covering of stucco painted – inscriptions too damaged to decipher paintings of god figures. Bones only found inside.	Position Extended
			S.D.
			Stufen Dynastic

Pottery			Other Objects	
Drawing	Type	Museum Number	Description	Museum Number

Grave Number	Position in Cemetery	Date Excavated	Photograph Number
30	2.55 × 4.25	21st Jan. 1905	

<table>
<tr><td rowspan="5">Sketch of Grave
</td><td colspan="2">Measurements
L: 1.10 m
W: 0.70 m</td><td>Bodies
one</td></tr>
<tr><td colspan="2" rowspan="2"></td><td>Sex
?</td></tr>
<tr><td>Disturbed
No</td></tr>
<tr><td colspan="2">Special Notes
E and f full of fine dark powder</td><td>Position
Head south
Face west</td></tr>
<tr><td colspan="2"></td><td>S.D. 55-76

Stufen
IId2-IIIa1
Late Gerzean</td></tr>
</table>

Pottery

Drawing	Type	Museum Number	Other Objects Description	Museum Number
a	? R55a	Sh. J1905.90 vase AM. 25.11.05.23 missing	broken palette	
b	? F88			
d	? R65c			
ε f	? L30B or L30c			
g h	cf. L7c	Bur. EG. 398 Sh. J1905.91		

Grave Number	Position in Cemetery	Date Excavated	Photograph Number
31	4.10 x 5.50	21st Jan. 1905	

Sketch of Grave	Measurements	Bodies

Measurements

Special Notes

Head lying on left side body twisted around

Bodies
One

Sex
?

Disturbed
Yes

Position
Head north Face east

S.D. 67-78

Stufen
IIIa 2 - IIIb Protodynastic

Pottery

Drawing	Type	Museum Number
a	L50A Strainer inside	W.E4033
b	L36k	
d small basin	?L18c	
c as lid to b)	?R24a	

Other Objects

Description	Museum Number

Grave Number	Position in Cemetery	Date Excavated	Photograph Number
32	7.65 × 9.50	21st Jan. 1905	H.30

Sketch of Grave	Measurements	Bodies
	L: 1.30 m W: 0.75 m	One

Sex: Female

Disturbed: No

Special Notes
Adult apparently buried face downwards in kneeling position, pelvis being quite back side up

Position
Head south
Face west
S.D. 45-78

Stufen
II d1-II d2
Late Gerzean

Pottery			Other Objects	
Drawing	Type	Museum Number	Description	Museum Number
b + c	? R76h		marble with inlaid eye type 45D	
d decorated with red spots	W3/W3G		black stone	
ε	? L53F		Two flints near right shoulder blade	
f + g	? R1b		Ball of carnelian and ? bread in front of face	
a	? R76h	AMS. E15644 (MU.1476)		

HIERAKONPOLIS FORT.   GARSTANG EXCAVATION,1905.   GRAVE RECORD

Grave Number	Position in Cemetery	Date Excavated	Photograph Number
33	7.00 to head × 9.00	21st Jan. 1905	

Sketch of Grave		Measurements	Bodies One

Measurements	Bodies
L: 0.90m	One
W: 0.50m	

	Sex Infant
	Disturbed No
Special Notes	
	Position ? Head north ? Face east
	S.D.? 43-54
	Stufen ? IId1-IId2 Gerzean

Pottery

Drawing		Type	Museum Number
a,b	fine glaze b slightly larger than a	? P45b	
·c		? P24k	LU.E4227
d		? D ware	
	in redim	? R67	
	dish	? R2bc	

Other Objects

Description	Museum Number
Two spindle whorls	one LU. E718
Small flint	LU. E.6623
Chip of stone vase and dish all above + arabic bead	

HIERAKONPOLIS FORT.   GARSTANG EXCAVATION,1905.   GRAVE RECORD

Grave Number	Position in Cemetery	Date Excavated	Photograph Number
34	10.20 x 11.85	21st Jan. 1905	H.89

Sketch of Grave	Measurements	Bodies
	L: 1.15 m W: 0.80 m	One
		Sex: ? Female
		Disturbed: Yes
	Special Notes: Body twisted in all directions and bones displaced	Position: Head south Face west S.D. 44-64
		Stufen II b Gerzean

Pottery

Drawing	Type	Museum Number	Other Objects — Description	Museum Number
decorated with spirals two handles.	D67J		b slate palette	
c	? 116F			
d coarse blackened top	? B76M			

Grave Number	Position in Cemetery	Date Excavated	Photograph Number
35	13.0 × 14.75	21st Jan. 1905	H.33, H.98

Sketch of Grave	Measurements	Bodies
	L: 1.15m W: 0.80m	One

Sex
? Female

Disturbed
No

Special Notes

Head upturned lying on left side

Position
Head south
Face west

S.D. 60-72

Stufen
IId2
Late Gerzean

Pottery

Drawing	Type	Museum Number
a, ε	W42	
c, n	R65d	
d decorated with dots and stripes	cf. F69p	LU.E3037
f decorated with spots	D63c	?LU.E6867
g	? R38	
J	R24a	
k, l, m	R81p	

Other Objects

Description	Museum Number
2 bone pins under head	One — LM.25.11.05.23
black pebble in hand	
Small flints copper pin pebble carnelian } under head	pebble LU.E721
h slate palette	

Grave Number	Position in Cemetery	Date Excavated	Photograph Number
36	11.20 x 13.10	21st Jan. 1905	H.35

Sketch of Grave	Measurements	Bodies
	L : 1.00	One
	W: 0.90	**Sex**
		? Female
		Disturbed
	Special Notes	Yes
		Position
		Head south Face west
		S.D. ?48-67
		Stufen IId1-IId2 Late Gerzean

slate palette under dish

Pottery

Drawing	Type	Museum Number	Other Objects Description	Museum Number
a — fine red glaze	? PR93d		slate palette	LU. E5381
b — red fine glaze	PR84H	Bol.44.05.3	perforated shell	LU. E2914
c	L16b	BM.42131		

Grave Number	Position in Cemetery	Date Excavated	Photograph Number
37	10.35 9.75 to corner	21st Jan. 1905	H.36

Sketch of Grave	Measurements	Bodies
		One
		Sex
		?
	95 cm deep	Disturbed
	Special Notes	No
	Very broken bones and twisted body	Position
		Head south Face west
		S.D. ?52-78
		Stufen
		?IId2 - IIIa1 Gerzean- Protodynastic

Pottery

Drawing	Type	Museum Number			Museum Number
a,c,e & g	?R24a			L R74G	Bolt. 44.05.22
d	?R26e				
h	?R24m				
i k small with remains inside		i.LM.25.11.0528 missing			
b	?L16B			P ?L16B	
f decorated with red paint	cf. W19 or WA3b				
m o like m but poor clay	?L7b				
n	?W2b				

Grave Number	Position in Cemetery	Date Excavated	Photograph Number
38	11.00 x 11.50 to corner	21st. Jan. 1905	

Sketch of Grave	Measurements	Bodies
		One

	D: 0.95 cm	**Sex** ?
		Disturbed No
	Special Notes	
		Position Head south Face west
		S.D. ?58-76
		Stufen ?IId2-IIIa1 Gerzean - Protodynastic

Pottery

Drawing	Type	Museum Number		Museum Number
	?L36K			
c	?R24a		remnant of palm leaf sealing & mud around rim.	
d broken	?R76g		?L30b	
g broken	?R34c		slate palette	LU. E5374

Grave Number	Position in Cemetery	Date Excavated	Photograph Number
39	13.00 × 13.10 to corner	21st Jan.1905	

Sketch of Grave	Measurements	Bodies
		None

slak palette

Measurements	
90 cm deep	Sex ?
	Disturbed Yes

Special Notes
Had traces of cover of matting
Between 38 and 39 was a wall built of rough stones as 38 had accidently exposed 39 and necessitated a re-burial

Position
?

S.D. ?42-78

Stufen
IId2 Late Gerzean

Pottery

Drawing	Type	Museum Number
b	?R24a	
c	?L16B	
d	?R66A	
E	?R85P	

Other Objects

Description	Museum Number
a traces of green ? type 455	

Grave Number	Position in Cemetery	Date Excavated	Photograph Number
40	? under wall	23rd Jan. 1905	

Sketch of Grave		Measurements	Bodies

Measurements:
Total length of body including head 60 cms.

	Value
Bodies	One
Sex	?
Disturbed	Yes
Position	?
S.D.	
Stufen	Dynastic

Special Notes

Burial in fairly good preservation skin well preserved, hands, feet. Burial however broken through the wall falling on it. Around the neck were several beads sacred eyes, also two earrings and another ring apparently on the string of beads - no trace of cloth

Pottery			Other Objects	
Drawing	Type	Museum Number	Description	Museum Number

Grave Number	Position in Cemetery	Date Excavated	Photograph Number
41		23rd Jan. 1905	

Sketch of Grave		Measurements 1.00 m long	Bodies One
			Sex Apparently male
			Disturbed No
		Special Notes Another small well preserved burial wrapped up in yellow cloth the border at the feet being made of red threads worked in the yellow, while on either side are blue threads. Bones sturdy & very small. Shell & eye amulet. Green glaze figure of Bes.	Position ?
			S.D.
			Stufen Dynastic

Pottery			Other Objects	
Drawing	Type	Museum Number	Description	Museum Number
			Shell - cowrie	LU. E2901
			Udjat eye, faience	LU. E252

HIERAKONPOLIS FORT.   GARSTANG EXCAVATION, 1905.   GRAVE RECORD

Grave Number	Position in Cemetery	Date Excavated	Photograph Number
42	600 to E. wall 3.75 to S. wall		H.37

Sketch of Grave		Measurements	Bodies

Measurements	Bodies
L: 1.50 m	One
W: 1.25 m	Sex
	? Male
	Disturbed
Special Notes	No
	Position
	Head east Face north
	S.D. 40-72
	Stufen IId1 - IId2 Late Gerzean

Pottery			Other Objects	
Drawing	Type	Museum Number	Description	Museum Number
W under Y	F32d	g= LU.E4051	under F palette P	
	P40c	y= LU.E4083	under d E + i palette Q	
	D1t	f= LU.E6865	under palette Q 2 red pebbles	
	D10c.dec. D8q	c= LU.E3032		
	P95b	x = LU.E4454		
	W42	L = ? Sw. W1048		

Grave Number	Position in Cemetery	Date Excavated	Photograph Number
43	5.00 to E.wall 4.00 to S.wall	23rd Jan. 1905	H.38

Sketch of Grave	Measurements	Bodies
	L: 1.30 m W: 0.85 m	One
		Sex ? Female
		Disturbed No
	Special Notes	
		Position Head south Face west S.D.?73-82
		Stufen ?IIIa2-IIIb Protodynastic - Dynasty I

Pottery			Other Objects	
Drawing	Type	Museum Number	Description	Museum Number
a	? Proto.63e			
b	? Proto.56E2			
c	? W61			
d	? W62			

HIERAKONPOLIS FORT.   GARSTANG EXCAVATION,1905.   GRAVE RECORD

Grave Number	Position in Cemetery	Date Excavated	Photograph Number
44	1.50 to S. wall 4.00 to E. wall	23rd Jan. 1905	

Sketch of Grave	Measurements	Bodies

	Measurements	Bodies
	0.80m square	One

Measurements

0.80m square

Bodies	One
Sex	Infant
Disturbed	Yes

Special Notes

Hair still on head
bones very disturbed
& broken.

Position	Head south Face west
S.D.?	55-81
Stufen	? IIc - IId 1 Gerzean

Pottery

Drawing	Type	Museum Number
a	? L53M	
b	D41b undecorated	L.U. E6095
c	? L7c	

Other Objects

Description	Museum Number
d — irregular slate palette	

Grave Number	Position in Cemetery	Date Excavated	Photograph Number
45	2.25 x 65 corner (rt.angle)	23rd Jan. 1905	

Sketch of Grave	Measurements	Bodies

Measurements

L: 0.90 m

W: 0.90 m

Bodies
Two

Sex
Child

Disturbed
Yes

Special Notes
Bones very broken
Under c was also
another burial the
head being at c
and the legs going
in west direction

Position
Head east
Face north

S.D.? 60-78

Stufen
? III a 2
Protodynastic

Pottery

Drawing

Type	Museum Number	Other Objects Description	Museum Number
? R 65 c			
? L 36 P			

HIERAKONPOLIS FORT.   GARSTANG EXCAVATION,1905.   GRAVE RECORD

Grave Number	Position in Cemetery	Date Excavated	Photograph Number
46	1.00 to E wall 5.10 to S.Wall	23rd Jan. 1905	

Sketch of Grave		Measurements	Bodies
		L: 0.75 m W: 0.60 m	One

	Measurements	Bodies
Sex		Infant

	Special Notes	Disturbed
		Yes

		Position
		Head south Face west
		S.D. ?31-56
		Stufen ?IIb Gerzean

Pottery			Other Objects	
Drawing	Type	Museum Number	Description	Museum Number
?a	P93a	Car. 75.776		

Grave Number	Position in Cemetery	Date Excavated	Photograph Number
47	5.00 to S.wall 4.25 to E.wall	23rd Jan. 1905	H.39

Sketch of Grave	Measurements	Bodies
	L: 1.65 m W: 1.00 m	One

Sex
? Female

Disturbed
No

Special Notes

Position
Head south Face west

S.D. ? 41-64

Stufen
? IIc - IId2 Gerzean

Pottery

Drawing	Type	Museum Number
b	?shape ⟩12b	
h	D67L	LU. E6433
K	? R84d	
j	? P24m	AMS. E15683 (MU.1475)

Other Objects

Description	Museum Number

HIERAKONPOLIS FORT.   GARSTANG EXCAVATION,1905.   GRAVE RECORD

Grave Number	Position in Cemetery	Date Excavated	Photograph Number
48	8.60 from S wall to mouth of pot 3.75 to E wall	23rd Jan. 1905	H.40

Sketch of Grave	Measurements	Bodies
	L: 0.63 m W: 0.60m	One

	Sex
	?

	Disturbed
	Yes

Special Notes	Position
A skull in pot a) which is broken	

	S.D.?40-65

	Stufen II d2 - III a 1 Late Gerzean- Protodynastic

Pottery

Drawing	Type	Museum Number	**Other Objects** Description	Museum Number
b or c	? P40c	Bol.44.05.12 on loan to Lin.(2140.25)		
a	? L40			

Grave Number	Position in Cemetery	Date Excavated	Photograph Number
49	9.75 to S.wall 2.40 to E.wall	23rd Jan. 1905	H.41

Sketch of Grave		Measurements	Bodies
		L: 0.65m	One

			Sex
		W: 0.45m	Child

			Disturbed
		Special Notes	No

		Few green glaze beads & white bone ones. 14 fragments.	Position Head south-west Face north-west
			S.D. ?80
			Stufen
			? Dynasty I

Pottery				Other Objects	
Drawing		Type	Museum Number	Description	Museum Number
	a	? Proto. 91 L		c) Slate palette	LU.E5380
	b	? Proto. 1j			

Grave Number	Position in Cemetery	Date Excavated	Photograph Number
50	1.75 to S. wall 3.25 to E.wall	23rd Jan. 1905	H.42

Sketch of Grave	Measurements	Bodies

Measurements

L: 1.50 m

W: 1.00 m

50 cm deep

Bodies
One

Sex
? Female

Disturbed
No

Special Notes

Bones very broken and old, lying on left side with hands before face, head covered with dark hair unplaited

Position

Head east
Face north
S.D.? 46-68

Stufen
? IIc - IId1
Gerzean

Pottery

Drawing	Type	Museum Number
Under pelvis decorated + bands of wavy lines	f cf.D10k	LU.E 6094
	a PR93c	LU.E 4431

Other Objects

Description	Museum Number
Broken spoon to north of head about 5 cm + below	LM. 25.11.05.47
Double bird slate palette type 67D	LM. 25.11.05.40

HIERAKONPOLIS FORT.   GARSTANG EXCAVATION,1905.   GRAVE RECORD

Grave Number	Position in Cemetery	Date Excavated	Photograph Number
51	3.00 to S. wall 9.50 to E. wall	23rd Jan. 1905	H45

Sketch of Grave	Measurements	Bodies
		One

		Sex
		? Female

		Disturbed
	Special Notes	No
	Under head was small remnant of wood which crumbled away on attempting to remove. Stone marked in drawing was simply rough + unworked.	**Position** Head north Face east S.D.? 55-73
		Stufen ? IId2-IIIa1 Late Gerzean

Pottery

Other Objects

Drawing	Type	Museum Number	Description	Museum Number
ε f g	? R84H		Dark beads with one flat bone circular bead	
a c	? R65c		d) slate palette	
b	L12c	Car. 75.772		

HIERAKONPOLIS FORT.   GARSTANG EXCAVATION,1905.   GRAVE RECORD

Grave Number	Position in Cemetery	Date Excavated	Photograph Number
52	2.00 to S.Wall 11.50 to E wall	23rd Jan. 1905	H.43

Sketch of Grave ↑	Measurements	Bodies
	L: 1.30 m W: 0.75 m	One
		Sex ?
		Disturbed No
	Special Notes	Position Head north Face east S.D. ?53-67
		Stufen ?IIc –IId1 Gerzean

Pottery

Drawing	Type	Museum Number
a	?L7b	AMS. E15668 (MU 1457)
c	R81	AMS. E15669 (MU 1474)
b	?L16g	

Other Objects

Description	Museum Number

Grave Number	Position in Cemetery	Date Excavated	Photograph Number
53	3.80 to S.wall 9.65 to bone along S.wall	23rd Jan. 1905	H.44

Sketch of Grave	Measurements	Bodies

Measurements

L: 1.25 m

W: 0.70 m

Special Notes

Small shell found under head very weak burial bones all broken

Bodies

One

Sex

? Female

Disturbed

No

Position

Head south Face west

S.D.? 52-76

Stufen

II a2 Late Gerzean

Pottery

Drawing	Type	Museum Number	Other Objects Description	Museum Number
c	? W43b			
d	? R84d			

HIERAKONPOLIS FORT.   GARSTANG EXCAVATION,1905. GRAVE RECORD

Grave Number	Position in Cemetery	Date Excavated	Photograph Number
54	2.00 to S. wall 8.25 to E. wall	25th Jan. 1905	

Sketch of Grave		Measurements	Bodies One
			Sex Infant
			Disturbed Yes
		Special Notes No bones but head and general direction of body given by fragments	Position Head south Face West
			S.D. ?37-67
			Stufen ?IId1 Gerzean

Pottery

Drawing	Type	Museum Number	Other Objects Description	Museum Number
a				
b irregular dark red glaze	PR93a	Bol.44.05.5		

HIERAKONPOLIS FORT.   GARSTANG EXCAVATION,1905.   GRAVE RECORD

Grave Number	Position in Cemetery	Date Excavated	Photograph Number
55		26th Jan. 1905	

Sketch of Grave		Measurements	Bodies
			none
			Sex
			Disturbed
		Special Notes	yes
			Position
			S.D.? 60-75
			Stufen ? II d2 - III a1 ? Late Gerzean

Pottery			Other Objects	
Drawing	Type	Museum Number	Description	Museum Number
dish found about 5 cm under present level upside down			Flints	
	? R38			
4 small dishes +small jar also found in redim				
broken in redim traces of red glaze small coarse pot	? R65c	a. LM.25.11.05.22 missing b.?LM.13.12.05.4 missing		

Grave Number	Position in Cemetery	Date Excavated	Photograph Number
56	Centre of Fort 21.00 to N. wall 14.20 to E. wall	26th Jan. 1905	H.86

Sketch of Grave	Measurements	Bodies
	0.30m below desert level 1.15 to lowest course of bricks from desert level	One

Measurements

0.30m below desert level
1.15 to lowest course of bricks from desert level

Special Notes

In excavating the area of visible brick masonry. Section: the brick wall about 80 cms, dark sand 1m and at bottom burial 56.

Bodies One

Sex ?

Disturbed No

Position Head south Face west
S.D.? 68-79

Stufen III a1-III b
Protodynastic - Dynasty I

Pottery

Drawing	Type	Museum Number		Museum Number
b small pot 3 ins	? Proto. 89 c-d		k 4 ins 393d dark red.	
e 8 in broken	? L19a		two pots to west of burial	
g dull brown about 18"	? L30K		? L31b	
de	? R26c		copper pin found under bones	
f 20in dark yellow	? Proto. 63F		c slate ? type 69B	
			Pebble W. EM19	

d) small beads, blue disc uniform, R. wrist

HIERAKONPOLIS FORT.   GARSTANG EXCAVATION, 1905.   GRAVE RECORD

Grave Number	Position in Cemetery	Date Excavated	Photograph Number
57	31.00 to N. wall 7.25 to W. wall	26th Jan. 1905	H.87

Sketch of Grave	Measurements	Bodies
a) pot broken above b ⇩	L: 1.30 m W: 0.50 m	One

		Sex
		? Female

	Special Notes	Disturbed
	Lying on left side with legs much drawn up	No

Position
Head south Face west

S.D. ? 77-78

Stufen IIIb Protodynastic – Dynastic I

Pottery

Drawing	Type	Museum Number	Other Objects Description	Museum Number
d a similar to c	? L 36h			
c	? Proto 70L			
right hand side uppermost pointed end to West & the back side faced the burial see the lines	? fire dog			

Grave Number	Position in Cemetery	Date Excavated	Photograph Number
58	near b1 and south of it	27th Jan. 1905	

Sketch of Grave		Measurements	Bodies None
			Sex
			Disturbed
		Special Notes 7 small pots all found in redim	Position
			S.D. ?42-81
			Stufen ?IId2-IIIa1 Gerzean - Protodynastic

Pottery			Other Objects	
Drawing	Type	Museum Number	Description	Museum Number
a	?Rbba	pot LM.25.11.05.21 missing		
b	? R63			
c	?P82b			
d	? R4b			
f	?R24a			
ε	?R54a			

Grave Number	Position in Cemetery	Date Excavated	Photograph Number
59	Door way of fort ·65 from S. side	27th Jan. 1905	

Sketch of Grave		Measurements	Bodies None
			Sex
			Disturbed
		Special Notes	Position
			S.D. ?34-46
			Stufen ?Ib Amratian

Pottery			Other Objects	
Drawing	Type	Museum Number	Description	Museum Number
black top pot fine glaze 10cm below redim	?B27f			
red glaze dish				

HIERAKONPOLIS FORT.   GARSTANG EXCAVATION, 1905.   GRAVE RECORD

Grave Number	Position in Cemetery	Date Excavated	Photograph Number
60	5.25 to W. wall 2.20 to S. wall of door	27th Jan. 1905	H.46

Sketch of Grave	Measurements	Bodies
↓	L: 1.40 m W: 0.80 m	One

Measurements
L: 1.40 m
W: 0.80 m

Bodies	One
Sex	?
Disturbed	No
Position	Head south
S.D.	77-81
Stufen	III b Dynasty I

Special Notes

Lying on its back arms right across body, left coincides with humerus
Remnants of hair on head

Pottery

Drawing	Type	Museum Number	Other Objects Description	Museum Number
a	W 80b			
b — fine large dish reddish colour + good glaze	? Proto.25d	Sw.W1047		
c	? Proto.63e			

Grave Number	Position in Cemetery	Date Excavated	Photograph Number
61	25.00 to N.wall 13.00 to E.wall	27th Jan. 1905	H.49

Sketch of Grave	Measurements	Bodies
		One

Measurements

Bodies One

Sex ?

Disturbed No

Special Notes
Bones very brittle unable to move without breaking

Position Head south Face west

S.D. 73-81

Stufen
III a2 - III b
Protodynastic
- Dynasty I

Pottery

Drawing	Type	Museum Number		Museum Number
a	Proto. 63j	Pot LM.16.11.06.41 missing	g	
c	? Proto. 3d		f	W55
d	? L31b		m	L33m
E	W61		n large deep basin broken	? Proto. 3N
h	h. ? Proto.1d			
k r P	krP.?Proto.1k			

b r c two dishes, b smaller

P found under pelvis

Grave Number	Position in Cemetery	Date Excavated	Photograph Number
62	17.75 to E.wall 33.25 to N.wall	27th Jan. 1905	H.47

Sketch of Grave	Measurements	Bodies
	L: 1.40 m W: 1.00 m	One

Sex ?Female

Disturbed No

Special Notes

Head of burial rested on a stone rough hewn Over head seemed to have been wood, decayed fragments remained, probably reeds

Position

Head south Face west

S.D. ? 77-79

Stufen

III a2 - III b
Protodynastic-Dynasty I

Pottery

Drawing	Type	Museum Number
a d	? Proto. 60f	
b ₊ c	? R24m	
f Small under pot E		
a found under a	? R24m	
k two L dishes remnants of mud - used as pot cover		
L	? R26a	

Other Objects

Description

Under L was another dish full of green fragments (cf. kohl?)

g slate palette

E slate palette

Museum Number
LU.5382

Grave Number	Position in Cemetery	Date Excavated	Photograph Number
63	21.75 to E.wall 33.25 to N.wall	27th Jan. 1905	H.88

Sketch of Grave	Measurements	Bodies
↙X	L: 1.20m W: 0.80m	One

	Sex
	?

	Disturbed
	No

Special Notes

Inside left hand were a
a string of beads
arranged in no
particular order or
symmetry, around neck
were also green glaze
beads , above head
was a broken bone
pin

Position	Head S-east
S.D. ?79	
Stufen	IIb Dynasty I

Pottery

Drawing	Type	Museum Number	Other Objects Description	Museum Number
a b	coarse pots whitened surface	?Proto.60e		

HIERAKONPOLIS FORT.   GARSTANG EXCAVATION,1905.   GRAVE RECORD

Grave Number	Position in Cemetery	Date Excavated	Photograph Number
64	2.00 to S.wall 4.20 to W. wall of door	27th Jan. 1905	

Sketch of Grave	Measurements	Bodies One

Sex ?

Disturbed ? No

Special Notes

Lying on right side body r pelvis lying on its face

Position Head north Face west

S.D. ?

Stufen ?

Pottery

Drawing

	Type	Museum Number	Other Objects Description	Museum Number

Grave Number	Position in Cemetery	Date Excavated	Photograph Number
65	In redîm	27th Jan. 1905	H.50

Sketch of Grave		Measurements	Bodies None
			Sex
			Disturbed
		Special Notes	Position
		near granite stones, pillar base	
			S.D. ?39-74
			Stufen ?IId2-IIIa1 Late Gerzean

Pottery			Other Objects	
Drawing	Type	Museum Number	Description	Museum Number
	? R26f	Vase LM.25.11.05.18 missing	Numerous flint flakes	one LU. E6637
	? R38			
pots all Weathered	R66p	Bol.44.05.28		
2 dishes				
oval dish	? F15b			

HIERAKONPOLIS FORT.   GARSTANG EXCAVATION,1905.   GRAVE RECORD

Grave Number	Position in Cemetery	Date Excavated	Photograph Number
66 cont.→	.50 to S.wall 6.85 to W.wall of door	28th Jan. 1905	H.96

Sketch of Grave	Measurements	Bodies
	L: 1.10m W: 0.75m	One

		Sex
		Child

	Special Notes	Disturbed
	Hair on head dark and not very long 2 pebbles – burnishers under arms	No

Position
? Head south Face West

S.D. ? 43-76

Stufen
II d 1 – II d 2 Gerzean

Pottery

Drawing	Type	Museum Number		Museum Number
a	? R81p		g h L	Bowl – LM. 30.86.7 Dish – LM.13.12.05.6 missing Vase – LM.13.12.05.9 missing
A to G	P75i	C. LU.E4052 E. LU.E6100	d e j ?B39b f	
Ʒ	W19	LU.E6859		
			k M,P,W1,W4 LTA W four dishes under Y S W2,W3	K. LU.E4279
c	? R84d		T ?R76g	

HIERAKONPOLIS FORT. GARSTANG EXCAVATION, 1905. GRAVE RECORD

Grave Number	Position in Cemetery	Date Excavated	Photograph Number
66 continued			

Sketch of Grave	Measurements	Bodies
		Sex
		Disturbed
	Special Notes	Position
		S.D.
		Stufen

Pottery

Drawing		Type	Museum Number
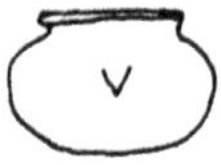 V			
 Y α		P40e	X or α LU.E4309
 Z			?LU.E4307
 β	black inside	?L16b	
 ∀		P95d	LU.E4053
 Δ	Δ under Y		

Other Objects

Description		Museum Number
 Q	? type 20c slate palettes	
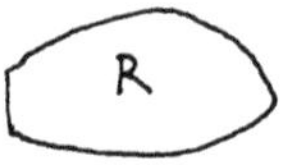 R	of type 46L	LU.E5338
	two bone hairpins under right arm	
	copper bracelet in right hand	LM.25.11.05.49
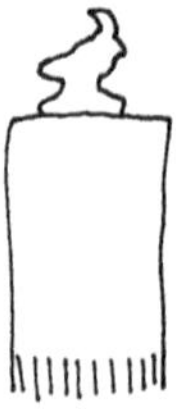	bone comb on head	LM.25.11.05.48
	flints	LU.E6610, E6617, E6620, E6622
	copper fish hook	LM.25.11.05.50
	clay beads south of R	
	varied beads at X	

Grave Number	Position in Cemetery	Date Excavated	Photograph Number
67	Redim in centre of fort near 74 r to south	28th Jan. 1905	

Sketch of Grave		Measurements	Bodies None
			Sex
			Disturbed
		Special Notes	Position
			S.D.
			Stufen

Pottery			Other Objects	
Drawing	Type	Museum Number	Description	Museum Number
a			Flint flakes	
b	rough hand made			
c	coarse			
d	coarse			
in 9 dishes variants of these two				
E				

Grave Number	Position in Cemetery	Date Excavated	Photograph Number
68	Burial under N. Wall of door	28th Jan. 1905	H.51, H.52, H.98

Sketch of Grave		Measurements	Bodies

Measurements
3.30 from E. side to E. corner
L: 2.50 m

W: 1.75 m

1.50 deep to old desert level
1.80 deep from last course of bricks

Special Notes

Bodies	One
Sex	?
Disturbed	No
Position	Head north Face west
S.D.	? 46-76
Stufen	? IId1 – IId2 Gerzean

Pottery

Drawing	Type	Museum Number	Other Objects Description	Museum Number
a c d l m	R84c-d	Bur. EG242		
b shapeless dish under c r d	R23D	? LU.E4663		
d broken				
decorated pot in shape of bird f	F69T	LU. E3036		
h variant of g	? W47g			
g k p l	? R26c			
Q				
R	? R38			

Grave Number	Position in Cemetery	Date Excavated	Photograph Number
69	11.25 to W.wall .60 in front of S.wall of door	29th Jan. 1905	H.53

Sketch of Grave	Measurements	Bodies
	L: 1.55m W: 1.25m	One

	Sex
	?

	Disturbed
Special Notes	No

Special Notes	Position
Bones very broken impossible to remove	Head north Face west
	S.D. ? 38-73
	Stufen ? IId1-IIIa1 Gerzean-Protodynastic

Pottery

Drawing	Type	Museum Number
	? W41	
	? P57a	
c	? R38	
d	Ɛ ? P93b	
Ɛ m	? R26c	
f g h	? R81s	

Other Objects

Description	Museum Number
K slate palettes	
N	LU.E5307
under k	LM.25.11.05.46b
4 shells and 4 pebbles under N	shell LU.E2906
under right hand crystal stained purple number of carnelian green glazed and bone beads also copper cylindrical bead.	

Grave Number	Position in Cemetery	Date Excavated	Photograph Number
70	Position of burial [sketch] n°70 k 60s — SE Corner of fort	29th Jan. 1905	H.54

Sketch of Grave	Measurements	Bodies
↓	Burial 1.30 to lower course of bricks lowest course of bricks .70 to old desert level L: 1.40 W: 1.10	One

	Sex
	? Male

	Disturbed
Special Notes	No

Position
Head south
Face west

S.D. 40-63

Stufen
IIc - IId1
Gerzean

Pottery			Other Objects	
Drawing	Type	Museum Number	Description	Museum Number
a b	R81		K & L bone knives 2 pebble burnished	LU.E7261 (one) ? bull's rib
g	D36 x D40m	? LU.E3031		
broken c	? R62			
f under	? R26e			
d E h	d ? R38			
E decorated in red	h ? P93d D63a	LU.E6855		

Grave Number	Position in Cemetery	Date Excavated	Photograph Number
71	corner line of s.wall of door	29th Jan. 1905	H.55

Sketch of Grave		Measurements	Bodies
		L: 1.30 m	One
		W: 0.80 m	**Sex** ?
		.30 — wall	**Disturbed** No
		Special Notes	**Position** Head south Face west
			S.D.? 52-64
			Stufen ? IId2 Gerzean

Pottery				Other Objects	
Drawing	Type	Museum Number		Description	Museum Number
a — red glaze	? P84A				
b — broken	? P24k				
c	? R76b				

HIERAKONPOLIS FORT.   GARSTANG EXCAVATION,1905.   GRAVE RECORD

Grave Number	Position in Cemetery	Date Excavated	Photograph Number
72	25.00 to corner N.wall 18.00 to corner E.wall	29th Jan. 1905	H.56

Sketch of Grave	Measurements	Bodies
	L: 1.35 W: 0.75	One
		Sex ? Female
		Disturbed No
	Special Notes	**Position** Head south Face west
		S.D. ? 75-79
		Stufen ? IIIa2 Protodynastic

Pottery			Other Objects	
Drawing	Type	Museum Number	Description	Museum Number
	W62	LU.E6088	thick slate palette	
	R6ba	WAS.A230	under head white marble	

Grave Number	Position in Cemetery	Date Excavated	Photograph Number
73	1.00 to gebel level 31.00 to N. wall 19.00 to E. wall	29th Jan. 1905	H.57

Sketch of Grave	Measurements	Bodies
	L: 1.60 m W: 1.00m	One

Sex

?

Disturbed

No

Special Notes

Bones very broken

Position
Head south
Face west

S.D. ?75-79

Stufen
? IIIa2 -IIIb
Protodynastic –
Dynasty I

Pottery

Drawing	Type	Museum Number	**Other Objects** Description	Museum Number
	?W55	Vase Glu.'23-33w		
	?R26f		thick palette with rim Sunk full of kohl	
	?W61			
	? Proto.63e			
	? Proto 60k			

Grave Number	Position in Cemetery	Date Excavated	Photograph Number
74	20.00 to N.wall 17.00 to W.wall	29th Jan.1905	H.58

Sketch of Grave	Measurements	Bodies
	L: 1.00m W: 0.80m	One

Measurements
L: 1.00m
W: 0.80m

Bodies One

Sex ?

Disturbed No

Special Notes

Position Head south Face west

S.D. 73-79

Stufen IIIa2 - IIIb
Protodynastic - Dynasty I

Pottery

Drawing	Type	Museum Number	Other Objects Description	Museum Number
a	? R2bf			
b				
c d	? W61			
E + dish under head / f	? L36a			

Grave Number	Position in Cemetery	Date Excavated	Photograph Number
75	18.00 to N. wall 16.50 to W. wall	29th Jan. 1905	

Sketch of Grave	Measurements	Bodies

Sketch of Grave

× 3 pots found   over here

Measurements	**Bodies**
L: 1.60 m	One
W: 0.75 m	**Sex** ?
	Disturbed No
Special Notes	**Position** Head east Face south
	S.D.? 71–77
	Stufen ? IIIa2 –IIIb Protodynastic

Pottery

Drawing

a

b
r
c

d

Type	Museum Number
?W47a	
?L33c	

Other Objects

Description	Museum Number
hairpin above a few beads found under head carnelian pendant r green glazed bead	

Grave Number	Position in Cemetery	Date Excavated	Photograph Number
76	9.75 to W.wall 19.50 to N.wall	29th Jan. 1905	H.59

Sketch of Grave	Measurements	Bodies
	L: 1.20 m W: 1.10 m	One

		Sex
		?

		Disturbed
	Special Notes	No

	Position
	Head east Face south
	S.D.? 73-79
	Stufen ? IIIa2 - IIIb Protodynastic - Dynasty I

Pottery

Drawing	Type	Museum Number			Museum Number
a	?L30p				
b	?L19p				
c	? Proto.45m	AMS.E15671 (MU 1477)	f	? Proto 60j	
d			ε	?L32A	
g+h	?R24m				

HIERAKONPOLIS FORT.   GARSTANG EXCAVATION,1905.   GRAVE RECORD

Grave Number	Position in Cemetery	Date Excavated	Photograph Number
77	0.85 north from S. corner 1.75 to enter S. wall of fort	30th Jan. 1905	

Sketch of Grave		Measurements	Bodies

Sketch of Grave

⇩

Measurements

L: 0.80m

W: 0.75m

(77) (78) S. corner
(79)

Special Notes

Bodies
One

Sex
?

Disturbed
No

Position
Head south
Face west

S.D.

Stufen
?IIc -IId2
Gerzean

Pottery

Drawing	Type	Museum Number	Other Objects Description	Museum Number
a	? R2bc			
b				
c				

Grave Number	Position in Cemetery	Date Excavated	Photograph Number
78	0.85 north from S. corner + touching wall	30th Jan.1905	H.60

Sketch of Grave	Measurements	Bodies

Measurements

78 S. corner of fort

L: 1.00m
W: 0.80m

Special Notes

Bodies: One

Sex: ?

Disturbed: No

Position: ? Head south west

S.D. ?

Stufen: ?IIc –IId2 Gerzean.

Pottery

Drawing

a — fine red glaze full of black dust r charcoal

Type: ?P40a

Museum Number: LM.25.11.05.32 missing

Other Objects

Description

Museum Number

HIERAKONPOLIS FORT.   GARSTANG EXCAVATION,1905. GRAVE RECORD

Grave Number	Position in Cemetery	Date Excavated	Photograph Number
79	3.10 to S. corner 0.75 to E. wall	30th Jan. 1905	

Sketch of Grave	Measurements	Bodies
	L: 1.60 m W: 1.00 m	One

		Sex
		?
		Disturbed
	Special Notes	No
		Position
		S.D.
		Stufen
		II d1 - II d2 Gerzean

Pottery

Drawing	Type	Museum Number	Other Objects Description	Museum Number
a	?R76h		few green glaze beads under head.	
c under a was c red glaze b same as c	?P93a	BM.42094		

HIERAKONPOLIS FORT.   GARSTANG EXCAVATION,1905.   GRAVE RECORD

Grave Number	Position in Cemetery	Date Excavated	Photograph Number
80	2.00 to N. side of 61 in straight line	30th Jan. 1905	

Sketch of Grave		Measurements	Bodies
		L: 0.60 m W: 0.35 m	One

	Sex
	Infant

	Disturbed
Special Notes	No

	Position
	Head south Face west
	S.D.
	Stufen

Pottery

Drawing	Type	Museum Number	**Other Objects** Description	Museum Number
			⬭ black bead	

HIERAKONPOLIS FORT.   GARSTANG EXCAVATION,1905.   GRAVE RECORD

Grave Number	Position in Cemetery	Date Excavated	Photograph Number
81	23.75 to W.wall 25.00 to N.wall	30th Jan.1905	H.61

Sketch of Grave	Measurements	Bodies
	1.50 deep to old desert level present level 1.00 above desert level L:1.75m W: 0.85m	One
		Sex ?Female
	Special Notes Bones very displaced	**Disturbed** No
		Position ?
		S.D.? 73-81
		Stufen IIIa2-IIIb Protodynastic - Dynasty I

Pottery

Other Objects

Drawing	Type	Museum Number	Description	Museum Number
all dishes broken	? L30p		near burial were several dishes and broken slate palette in redim few green glaze beads under head.	
as cover to g which was under & coated with mud	d. W47a	BM.42081		
	f ?L16b			
	g .? L36k			

Grave Number	Position in Cemetery	Date Excavated	Photograph Number
82	21.00 to W. wall 19.25 to N. wall	30th Jan. 1905	

Sketch of Grave		Measurements	Bodies
		L: 1.30m W: 0.75m	One

			Sex
			?

	Special Notes	Disturbed
	Burial on its face head lying on right side	?No

Position
Head north Face east

S.D. ?73-79

Stufen
?IIIa2-IIIb Protodynastic- Dynasty I

Pottery			Other Objects	
Drawing	Type	Museum Number	Description	Museum Number
a	?L30p	Gla'23-33v		

Grave Number	Position in Cemetery	Date Excavated	Photograph Number
83	19.75 to W. wall 17.00 to N. wall	30th Jan. 1905	

Sketch of Grave	Measurements	Bodies
	L: 1.25 m W: 0.70 m .45 below old desert level	One

Measurements

L: 1.25 m

W: 0.70 m

.45 below old desert level

Bodies: One

Sex: ?

Disturbed: No

Special Notes

Legs bent up over chest, head under palette

Position: Head south

S.D.? 73-79

Stufen: ? III a 2 Protodynastic

Pottery			Other Objects	
Drawing	Type	Museum Number	Description	Museum Number
	?W61		[a] slate palette	
			black pebble over b in left hand was bone pin few green beads under head.	LÚ. E720

HIERAKONPOLIS FORT.   GARSTANG EXCAVATION,1905.   GRAVE RECORD

Grave Number	Position in Cemetery	Date Excavated	Photograph Number
84	19.00 to W.wall 16.50 to N.wall	30th Jan. 1905	

Sketch of Grave	Measurements	Bodies
	L: 1.20 m	One

	Measurements	Bodies
	W: 0.80 m	**Sex** ?
	. 5 under old desert level to top of pot	**Disturbed** Yes
	Special Notes	
	no head found apparently lying on his face	**Position**
		S.D. ?75-79
		Stufen ?IIIa2-IIIb Protodynastic - Dynasty I

Pottery

Drawing	Type	Museum Number	Other Objects Description	Museum Number
a b	?L30p		bone pendant	
c	?L36k			
d				

Grave Number	Position in Cemetery	Date Excavated	Photograph Number
85	.75 from outside wall S of S. corner of door .65 from SE corner of door southwards	30th Jan. 1905	H.62

Sketch of Grave	Measurements	Bodies None
		Sex
	Special Notes	Disturbed
		Position
		S.D. ?35-67
		Stufen ?IIc -IId2 Gerzean

Pottery			Other Objects	
Drawing	Type	Museum Number	Description	Museum Number
∧ c 75 b <.50 d a fine red glaze vase ∨ c d blackened poor work	?RB1c ?P4/c P22b	Bol.44.05.33		

HIERAKONPOLIS FORT.   GARSTANG EXCAVATION,1905.   GRAVE RECORD

Grave Number	Position in Cemetery	Date Excavated	Photograph Number
86/86A	In front to S of 85		

Sketch of Grave		Measurements	Bodies
			Sex
			Disturbed
		Special Notes Large numbers of hard marl pots 24 or more 86A To E of 79 under outer wall was burial lying full length hands at side, head to South, direction similar to outer wall	Position
			S.D.
			Stufen ? Dynastic

Pottery			Other Objects	
Drawing	Type	Museum Number	Description	Museum Number

HIERAKONPOLIS FORT.   GARSTANG EXCAVATION,1905.   GRAVE RECORD

Grave Number	Position in Cemetery	Date Excavated	Photograph Number
87	1.80 to outer Southernmost corner of fort	30th Jan. 1905	

Sketch of Grave	Measurements	Bodies
	L: 1.75 m	One
	W: 1.00 m	Sex
	O←→ 1.80	?
		Disturbed
	Special Notes	No
	Bones broken	Position Head north Face west
		S.D. ?43-72
		Stufen ?IId2 -IIIa1 Gerzean

Pottery			Other Objects	
Drawing	Type	Museum Number	Description	Museum Number
a	P40e	W.E6084	flints under head bitumen in eyes and head	
b				
c	?R 57c	AMS.E15651 (MU 1454)		
d				

Grave Number	Position in Cemetery	Date Excavated	Photograph Number
88	16.50 to E. wall 29.25 to N. wall	30th Jan. 1905	H.64, H.65

Sketch of Grave	Measurements	Bodies

southern burial

bone partially displaced through falling brickwork

Measurements

L: 1.20 m

W: 0.90 m

Special Notes

Bodies	One
Sex	Child
Disturbed	Yes
Position	Head south
S.D. ? 42-81	
Stufen	? II d2 - IIIa2 Gerzean - Protodynastic

Pottery

Other Objects

Drawing	Type	Museum Number	Description	Museum Number
a	? P95b		2 beads only found under head one Carnelian + one green glaze	
b	L36a	Bla.NN	d black stone	
c	? R24a			
ε	? R26a			
f	? R24a			

Grave Number	Position in Cemetery	Date Excavated	Photograph Number
89	16.40 to E.wall joins 88 on N.side	30th Jan. 1905	H.65 H.64

Sketch of Grave	Measurements	Bodies
	L: 1.00m W: 1.00m	One

		Sex ?
		Disturbed Yes
	Special Notes	**Position** Head south Face west
	Burial broken by fall of wall	
	Photograph also shows brick courses in centre of fort	S.D.?73-79
		Stufen IIIa2-IIIb Protodynastic- Dynasty I

Pottery

Drawing	Type	Museum Number	Other Objects Description	Museum Number
a broken	?L36n			
b c white Surface	? W51a			
ε	?L30p			
d small variant of b & c				

Grave Number	Position in Cemetery	Date Excavated	Photograph Number
90	2.50 to S. wall of fort	30th	H.66, H.67

Sketch of Grave	Measurements	Bodies
	L: 1.15 m W: 0.80 m	One

		Sex
		Child

	Special Notes	**Disturbed**
		No

Position
Head south
Face west

S.D. ?42-72

Stufen
IIc – IId2
Gerzean

Pottery			Other Objects	
Drawing	Type	Museum Number	Description	Museum Number
a,b rough pots one inside the other	?R66p	RISW.AX121.11	2 ? bone pendants & beads found X	
c same as a+b but fine red glaze	c. ?P95b		E cf. 40H	LIV.E5341
d	? P1a		broken shell under head	
f			bronze bracelet on right wrist over 90m in redtim fine flint knife (ng tht) beads found under thigh.	

Grave Number	Position in Cemetery	Date Excavated	Photograph Number
91	20.75 to W.wall 14.00 to N.wall	30th Jan.1905	H.68

Sketch of Grave	Measurements	Bodies
	L: 1.00 m W: 0.80 m	One

Remains of fair hair on skull over body several hand made dishes one apparently contained kohl

Special Notes

Burial under flat stones which were found at angle of about 45° over burial, over the head & under the stones were 2 pots & over the stones at the head was one pot and at the feet another

Sex	?
Disturbed	No
Position	Head east Face south
S.D.	?58-81
Stufen	?IIIa2 -IIIb Protodynastic

Pottery

Drawing	Type	Museum Number
a b d	?L36a	
a + c much broken ·b under present level		
h		
broken under x + same as E	?W61	
g very broken		
h very broken		

Other Objects

Description	Museum Number
slate palette under stone	LU. E5310
trace of red paint in centre, pebble (brown) near palette to E green glazed beads Carnelian + others on skull	
under right arm another palette	LM.13.12.05.14
	Murex shell LU·E2902

Grave Number	Position in Cemetery	Date Excavated	Photograph Number
92	3.00 to N. corner of door		H.69

Sketch of Grave	Measurements	Bodies

Measurements

L: 1.35 m
W: 0.80 m
.80 deep

3.00

Bodies
One

Sex
? Male

Disturbed
No

Special Notes

Position
Head south west
Face east

S.D. ?35-76

Stufen
?IIc – IId2
Gerzean

Pottery

Drawing	Type	Museum Number
a		
b / c / e	?b cf L53a c rE ? R84	Bur. EG248
g	? P93d	
d / f	? W13	
h black top	B58a	LU. E6203

Other Objects

Description	Museum Number

HIERAKONPOLIS FORT.   GARSTANG EXCAVATION,1905.   GRAVE RECORD

Grave Number	Position in Cemetery	Date Excavated	Photograph Number
93	to N. corner of door .50 in straight line See 92	1st Feb. 1905	H.70

Sketch of Grave	Measurements	Bodies
X	N corner 94 40°	One

Measurements

L: 1.30 m
W: 0.65 m

Special Notes

Lying on back. Hair on head long + black

Bodies	One
Sex	? Male
Disturbed	No
Position	Heads west Face east
S.D. ?	36-68
Stufen	IIc - IId2 Gerzean

Pottery

Drawing	Type	Museum Number
a	? R69c	
b	? R76d	Bur. EG339 rim sherd
c d similar to c but smaller	? R69d	

Other Objects

Description	Museum Number

Grave Number	Position in Cemetery	Date Excavated	Photograph Number
94	See 93	1st. Feb. 1905	H.22

Sketch of Grave	Measurements	Bodies

		Bodies Four
		Sex Children
		Disturbed No
	Special Notes	
	Four small burials all lying on left side one being at feet and facing other three.	Position
		S.D.?52-76
		Stufen ? II d1 - II d2 Gerzean

Pottery

Drawing

	Type	Museum Number
(a)	? R67	
(b)	? R84	

Other Objects

Description

Under C's head were 3 beads one carnelian and two clay beads also cylindrical.

Museum Number

HIERAKONPOLIS FORT.   GARSTANG EXCAVATION,1905.   GRAVE RECORD

Grave Number	Position in Cemetery	Date Excavated	Photograph Number
95	13.00 to E.wall 32.00 to N.wall	1st. Feb. 1905	H.71

Sketch of Grave		Measurements	Bodies
			One
			Sex ?
			Disturbed No
		Special Notes	**Position** Head south Face west S.D. ?79
			Stufen ?IIIa2-IIIb Protodynastic - Dynasty I

Pottery

Drawing	Type	Museum Number
a light yellowish pot	?L42	
b c d	?Proto.60j	LM.16.11.06.136 missing

Other Objects

Description	Museum Number
E square slate palette	

Grave Number	Position in Cemetery	Date Excavated	Photograph Number
96	16.50 to E.wall 23.00 to N.wall	1st Feb. 1905	H.72

Sketch of Grave		Measurements	Bodies

Sketch of Grave

Measurements

L: 1.40 m
W: 1.00 m

Bodies

One

Sex

?

Disturbed

No

Special Notes

Position
Head north
Face east

S.D. ?71-79

Stufen
?III a2 -III b
Protodynastic-
Dynasty I

Pottery

Drawing

b + c poor dishes

Type

E ? L30p
h ? L36k

? W51 a

Museum Number

Other Objects

Description

x small pebble

slate palette
m   cf 45B

few green glaze beads
+ broken pin on head

Museum Number

LU.E5339

Grave Number	Position in Cemetery	Date Excavated	Photograph Number
97	21.50 to N.wall 17.10 to E.wall	1st Feb. 1905	H.73

Sketch of Grave	Measurements	Bodies
	L: 1.80m W: 1.25m	One

	Sex
	?

Special Notes	Disturbed
L: 1.50m W: 1.25m	No

	Position
	Head south-west Face north

S.D. ? 58-81

Stufen
IIIb
Protodynastic
- Dynasty I

Pottery

Drawing	Type	Museum Number
a	? L59c	
b h k +m	C as cover over b ? L36a	
d + c under c		Dish LM.25.11.05.30 missing
g +h dishes like d		
f. With scratching	f. Proto. 45M	WAS. A228

near 97 to N good red glaze

Other Objects

Description	Museum Number

Grave Number	Position in Cemetery	Date Excavated	Photograph Number
98	3.00 from N. corner of door to S. of burial	2nd. Feb. 1905	

Sketch of Grave		Measurements	Bodies
		N corner / 3.00 / passage / △98 / Wall	One

Sketch of Grave

E.wall

Measurements

N corner
3.00
passage △98
Wall

L: 0.80m
W: 0.40m

Special Notes
Burial in broken pot doubled up and lying on right side.

Bodies	One
Sex	?
Disturbed	No
Position	Head east Face south
S.D.	?40-70
Stufen	?IIb-IId2 Gerzean

Pottery

Other Objects

Drawing	Type	Museum Number	Description	Museum Number
a	? R67		On right wrist - copper bracelet (broken)	
b · fine red glaze	?P93d		Below pelvis another copper bracelet (unbroken) necklace of pierced shells (white like periwinkles) and cowries above left hand.	LU. E807
c				
d red glaze	?P22b		slate palette	

Grave Number	Position in Cemetery	Date Excavated	Photograph Number
99	1.60 to outer N. corner of door	2nd . Feb . 1905	

Sketch of Grave		Measurements	Bodies

Measurements

L: 1.75m
W: 0.90m

Special Notes

Head and rest of body found in redim disturbed probably by diggers burrowing under wall of fort

Bodies
One

Sex
?

Disturbed
Yes

Position
Head? once northwest

S.D. ?52 -76

Stufen
?IId1 -IId2 Gerzean

Pottery

Drawing	Type	Museum Number
a	? R67	
b,c frg	? R8½d	
ε	? R 38	

Other Objects

Description	Museum Number
Slate palette	
dark brown pebble	

Grave Number	Position in Cemetery	Date Excavated	Photograph Number
100	Opposite 96 1.85m to E of it	2nd Feb .1905	

Sketch of Grave	Measurements	Bodies

Sketch of Grave	Measurements L: 0.70 m W: 0.45m	**Bodies** One
		Sex ?
	Special Notes Burial apparently on desert level	**Disturbed** No
		Position Head south Face west
		S.D. ?
		Stufen ?

Pottery

Drawing

⌐a⌐ broken

	Type	Museum Number

Other Objects

Description

Museum Number

Grave Number	Position in Cemetery	Date Excavated	Photograph Number
101	24.00 to N. corner 24.50 to E. corner	2nd. Feb. 1905	H.74

Sketch of Grave	Measurements	Bodies

	Measurements	Bodies
	L: 1.75m W: 1.00m	One
		Sex ?
		Disturbed No
	Special Notes	Position Head south Face west S.D.? 73-81
	b,k,m full of dark earth	Stufen IIa2-IIIb Protodynastic -Dynasty I

Pottery

Drawing	Type	Museum Number	Description	Museum Number
a 2 bands of wave pattern in dark red	cf Proto. 94k	LU. E4539	few beads under right arm	
b	b. ? L36a			
c				
e				
f	? R2ba			
g h	? W61			
k m	? L36a			

Other Objects

HIERAKONPOLIS FORT.   GARSTANG EXCAVATION,1905.   GRAVE RECORD

Grave Number	Position in Cemetery	Date Excavated	Photograph Number
102	20.00 to N·wall 22.00 to W·wall	2nd·Feb·1905	

Sketch of Grave		Measurements	Bodies
		L: 1·30m W: 0·80m	One
			Sex
			?
			Disturbed
		Special Notes	No
			Position Head east Face south
			S.D.? 73-79
			Stufen IIIa2 - IIIb Protodynastic - Dynasty I

Pottery			Other Objects	
Drawing	Type	Museum Number	Description	Museum Number
a	?L36n		under n brown pebble	
b	?L30p		x bone bracelets under right arm	5 - LM.13·12.05.38 1 - shell LU.E7262
c red glaze				
d t u v	?R24m	AMS.E15630 (CMU1480)	slate palette	
e	R?W51a			
R			o had Kohl inside	
h				
K red glaze				
S red glaze	Sof. P91	?LU.E4031		
m				
n,o				

Grave Number	Position in Cemetery	Date Excavated	Photograph Number
103	27.00 to E.wall 20.75 to N. wall	2nd. Feb.1905	

Sketch of Grave	Measurements	Bodies

	Measurements	Bodies
	L: 1.50m W: 0.90m	One
		Sex
		Child
		Disturbed
	Special Notes	No
	Inside P were remnants of kohl	Position Head east Face south
		S.D. ?57-81
		Stufen ?IId2-IIIb Protodynastic

Pottery

Other Objects

Drawing	Type	Museum Number	Description	Museum Number
a b c	?L30p		under head four cylindrical carnelian beads, pieces of kohl + burnished brown pebble a,b,c full of dark earth Q + k lighter earth ε + f full of sand	
h				
n	R24m	AMS.E15681 (MU 1473)		
R broken dish like N	?L43p			
d				
ε f	?L36a			
k a	?W43b		M slate palette	
g red glaze	P97k streak burnished	BM.42082		

Grave Number	Position in Cemetery	Date Excavated	Photograph Number
104		2nd Feb. 1905	

Sketch of Grave	Measurements	Bodies
	1.00 deep	One

		Sex
		?
		Disturbed
	Special Notes	Yes
	Buried lying on his back, head found lying above burial about 0.20m and the jaw under, the forearms were at c to south of head	Position Head once south Face ? west
		S.D. ?58-81
		Stufen ? IIIa2-IIIb Protodynastic - Dynasty I

Pottery

Other Objects

Drawing	Type	Museum Number	Description	Museum Number
a b b larger than a	?L36a			

Grave Number	Position in Cemetery	Date Excavated	Photograph Number
105	14.75 to W.wall 15.25 to N.wall	2nd Feb. 1905	

Sketch of Grave	Measurements	Bodies
	L: 1.25 m W: 0.80 m	One

Measurements
L: 1.25 m
W: 0.80 m

Sex ?

Disturbed ?

Special Notes

Lying on left side
No pots or beads

Position
Head south
Face west

S.D. ?

Stufen ?

Pottery

Drawing   Type   Museum Number

Other Objects

Description   Museum Number

Grave Number	Position in Cemetery	Date Excavated	Photograph Number
106	14.00 to N.wall 22.50 to w. wall	2nd Feb. 1905	

Sketch of Grave	Measurements	Bodies

Sketch of Grave	Measurements	**Bodies** One
	L: 1.00m	**Sex** ?
	W: 0.40 m	
	0.40 m below surface	**Disturbed** Yes
	Special Notes Adult lying on face. Head removed, left arm under body.	**Position** Head once south
		S.D. ? 73-79
		Stufen IIIa2-IIIb Protodynastic-Dynasty I

Pottery

Drawing	Type	Museum Number	Other Objects Description	Museum Number
a + b two hand made dishes full of mud				
c d very broken	?L30p	Bir. 129'56 (Ex. VrA.582.1905)		
ε dish also broken				

Grave Number	Position in Cemetery	Date Excavated	Photograph Number
107 Cont.↗	?	2nd. Feb. 1905	H.75 H.76

Sketch of Grave skull	Measurements	Bodies Two
		Sex ?
		Disturbed No
	Special Notes	Position a - Head south Face west
	lower burial lying on back with left hand over skull & dish over right arm & leg	S.D. ?73-80
		Stufen ? IIIa2-IIIb Protodynastic - Dynasty I

Pottery

Drawing	Type	Museum Number	**Other Objects** Description	Museum Number
			⟨η⟩ slate palette	??LU5344
	g. Proto.5f	BM. 42132		
	m- R24M	Bol. 44.05.6		
under w broken		Pottery disc Sh. J. 1905.93		

Grave Number	Position in Cemetery	Date Excavated	Photograph Number
107 continued			

Sketch of Grave	Measurements	Bodies

a
upper burial

lower burial

		Sex
		Disturbed
	Special Notes	Position
		S.D.
		Stufen

Pottery

Drawing	Type	Museum Number	Special Notes	Museum Number
W Z	W. of. L34b and Proto.72g but thinner	LU.E 6116	5 ? L30p	
X Y θ B	Z Proto. 70m.	RISW. AX121.5		
	β proto.70p	?LU.E 6116	≤ N 3	
under T		Vase LM.16.11.06.135 missing		
Δ	Δ Proto. 73f	WAS. A227		
4	4. Proto. 4tj	WAS. A228		

HIERAKONPOLIS FORT.   GARSTANG EXCAVATION,1905.   GRAVE RECORD

Grave Number	Position in Cemetery	Date Excavated	Photograph Number
108	18.50 to N.wall 25.50 to E.wall	2nd. Feb. 1905	H.95

Sketch of Grave	Measurements	Bodies
	L: 1.25 m W: 0.80m	One

		Sex
		? Male

		Disturbed
	Special Notes	No

		Position
		Head south-east Face west

| | | S.D. ?58-81 |

		Stufen
		IIIa2 – IIIb Protodynastic- Dynasty I

Pottery

Drawing	Type	Museum Number	Description	Museum Number
a b c d	?L36a		number of small beads green glazed rcarnelian	
3 pieces of broken dish				

Other Objects

Grave Number	Position in Cemetery	Date Excavated	Photograph Number
109	20.25 to E. wall 17.00 to N. wall	2nd. Feb. 1905	

Sketch of Grave	Measurements	Bodies
	L: 1.35 m W: 1.00 m	One

	Sex
	?

	Disturbed
Special Notes	No

Position
Head south Face west

S.D. ? 75-79

Stufen
IIIa2 - IIIb Protodynastic - Dynasty I

Pottery

Drawing	Type	Museum Number
a decorated with black stripes red ground	? W62	
c similar to a but under coated + yellow ground		
b	? L36a	

Other Objects

Description	Museum Number

HIERAKONPOLIS FORT.   GARSTANG EXCAVATION, 1905.   GRAVE RECORD

Grave Number	Position in Cemetery	Date Excavated	Photograph Number
110	W. side wall see 111	2nd. Feb. 1905	H:77, H:78

Sketch of Grave		Measurements	Bodies
		L: 2.00 m	One
		W: 0.60 m	Sex
			?
			Disturbed
			No
		Special Notes	Position
		Lying on face	Head south
			S.D.
			Stufen
			? Dynastic

right arm

(a)

Pottery			Other Objects	
Drawing	Type	Museum Number	Description	Museum Number
(a)			Carnelian cylindrical beads + pendant	

Grave Number	Position in Cemetery	Date Excavated	Photograph Number
111	in middle of w.side of 110 20.50 to E.wall 19.00 to N.wall	3rd. Feb .1905	H.78

Sketch of Grave	Measurements	Bodies
	L: 1.30 m W: 0.80m	One

		Sex
		?

	Special Notes	Disturbed
		?

		Position Head south Face west
		S.D. ?
		Stufen ?

Pottery			Other Objects	
Drawing	Type	Museum Number	Description	Museum Number
			Slate palette	

Grave Number	Position in Cemetery	Date Excavated	Photograph Number
112	16.60 to E. wall 17.00 to N. wall	8th . Feb. 1905	

Sketch of Grave		Measurements	Bodies
		L: 1.60 m W: 1.20 m	One
			Sex
			?
			Disturbed
		Special Notes	No
			Position Head south Face west
			S.D.? 75-79
			Stufen ? IIIa2-IIIb Protodynastic-Dynasty I

Pottery

Other Objects

Drawing	Type	Museum Number	Description	Museum Number
a	? Proto. 60j		broken slate palette	
			pieces of alabaster dish	
b	? L42	?LM. 25.11.05.20 missing		
e	? R24m			
c	? R67			

HIERAKONPOLIS FORT.   GARSTANG EXCAVATION,1905. GRAVE RECORD

Grave Number	Position in Cemetery	Date Excavated	Photograph Number
113	18.50 to E.wall 18.75 to W.wall	3rd .Feb. 1905	

Sketch of Grave	Measurements	Bodies
	L: 1.00 m W: 0.60 m	One

	Measurements	Sex
		?

		Disturbed
	Special Notes	?
	Burial on desert level no deposits	Position Head south Face west
		S.D. ?
		Stufen ?

Pottery			Other Objects	
Drawing	Type	Museum Number	Description	Museum Number

HIERAKONPOLIS FORT.   GARSTANG EXCAVATION,1905.   GRAVE RECORD

Grave Number	Position in Cemetery	Date Excavated	Photograph Number
114	?	3rd Feb. 1905	

Sketch of Grave	Measurements	Bodies

	0. 50m below desert level L: 1.30 m W: 0.75m	One
		Sex ?
		Disturbed No
	Special Notes	Position Head east Face south S.D. ?75-79
		Stufen ?IIIa2 Protodynastic

Pottery			Other Objects	
Drawing	Type	Museum Number	Description	Museum Number
a	?R26.			
b				
c	?W62			

Grave Number	Position in Cemetery	Date Excavated	Photograph Number
115	22.00 from E.wall 20.90 from N.wall	3rd. Feb. 1905	

Sketch of Grave	Measurements	Bodies
	L: 1.50 m W: 1.00 m 1.30 below desert level	One

		Sex
		?

		Disturbed
	Special Notes	No
	Above head to south bone hair pin, few carnelian beads Under head portions of 2 broken bone pins	**Position** Head south Face west
		S.D. ?73-78
		Stufen ?IIIa2-IIIb Protodynastic - Dynasty I

Pottery

Drawing	Type	Museum Number	Other Objects	
			Description	Museum Number
a+b	?L3br		See special notes	
Contained sand			x brown pebble	
c+d	?L30p		◻ k slate palette	
g+h	?R24m		Bone hair pin	LM.25.11.05.4bc
c+f	?W55			

Grave Number	Position in Cemetery	Date Excavated	Photograph Number
116	9.00 to E.wall 11.00 to N.wall	3rd. Feb. 1905	

Sketch of Grave	Measurements	Bodies
	L: 0.95 m	One
	W: 0.55 m	Sex
	0.60 m below present level	?
	present level, 2.20 above old desert	Disturbed
	Special Notes	Yes
	Burial without head	Position [Head] south Face west
		S.D. ? 77
		Stufen ? IIIb Protodynastic

Pottery			Other Objects	
Drawing	Type	Museum Number	Description	Museum Number
a, b	? Prot. 63j			
in redim near grave				
black earth inside				

Grave Number	Position in Cemetery	Date Excavated	Photograph Number
117	Burial unter W. Wall, 20.00 from N. corner	3rd. Feb. 1905	

Sketch of Grave	Measurements 1.10m long 0.30m wide	Bodies One

		Sex ?
	Special Notes Buried in yellow coarse Woollen(?) outer garments decorated with red, blue Border, inside garment of linen + with finer weaving Body well preserved. Head also wrapped up. Wall of fort 1.20m above desert level, this burial on old desert level	Disturbed No
		Position Head to South
		S.D.
		Stufen Dynastic

Pottery			Other Objects	
Drawing	Type	Museum Number	Description	Museum Number

HIERAKONPOLIS FORT.   GARSTANG EXCAVATION,1905.   GRAVE RECORD

Grave Number	Position in Cemetery	Date Excavated	Photograph Number
118	Under W. wall 23.00 from N.wall		

Sketch of Grave	Measurements	Bodies

	Measurements L: 1.80 m W: 0.45 m	Bodies One
		Sex ?
		Disturbed No
	Special Notes At the head (S.end) pot with a dish inside. Mummified.	Position Head south
		S.D.
		Stufen Dynastic

Pottery Drawing	Type	Museum Number	Other Objects Description	Museum Number

Grave Number	Position in Cemetery	Date Excavated	Photograph Number
119	17.50 to E. wall 14.50 to N. wall	3rd. Feb. 1905	

Sketch of Grave	Measurements	Bodies

Measurements
L : 1.20 m
W : 0.50 m

Bodies
One

Sex
?

Disturbed
No

Special Notes
On right wrist 3 bone bracelets and on left arm 3 ditto, left arm being straight down and hands under pelvis. Beads found strung as tho' necklace and in right arm near face, around neck dark carnelian beads

Position
Head south
Face west

S.D. ? 71-81

Stufen
? IIIa2 - IIIb
Protodynastic -
Dynasty I

Pottery

Drawing	Type	Museum Number
	a, b, c ? L30p	
	E ? R24m	
	f ? R26a	
	? W51a	
	? L36a	
	L16b	RISW. AX121.6

Other Objects

Description	Museum Number
Beads	

carn, bl.green, carn. ad. lib
2 carnelian, 7 green,
8 carnelian, 5 green
5 carnelian, 4 green

m   Slate palette

Grave Number	Position in Cemetery	Date Excavated	Photograph Number
120		3rd Feb. 1905	

Sketch of Grave			Measurements	Bodies

Bodies: None

Sex:

Disturbed:

Special Notes

Position:

S.D.

Stufen: ?Protodynastic

Pottery			Other Objects	
Drawing	Type	Museum Number	Description	Museum Number

portion of slate palette

2 dishes

hand made dish

Shell
1 bead gr. glaze

Beads + shells
LM. 25. 11. 05. 51

Grave Number	Position in Cemetery	Date Excavated	Photograph Number
121		3rd. Feb. 1905	

Sketch of Grave		Measurements	Bodies None
			Sex
			Disturbed
		Special Notes	Position
			S.D. ?42-81
			Stufen ?IIIa2 - IIIb

Pottery			Other Objects	
Drawing	Type	Museum Number	Description	Museum Number
	?L16b			
	?R24a			
& fragments of dishes				

HIERAKONPOLIS FORT.   GARSTANG EXCAVATION,1905.   GRAVE RECORD

Grave Number	Position in Cemetery	Date Excavated	Photograph Number
122	20.00 to E.wall 11.50 to N.wall	3rd. Feb. 1905	

Sketch of Grave	Measurements	Bodies
	L: 1.30 m W. 0.90 m	One

		Sex
		?

		Disturbed
	Special Notes	Yes
	Bones displaced	

		Position Head once South

S.D. ?73-78

Stufen
IIIa2-IIIb
Protodynastic

Pottery			Other Objects	
Drawing	Type	Museum Number	Description	Museum Number
a b + c	? L36a			
d + ε	cf. L30s			

Grave Number	Position in Cemetery	Date Excavated	Photograph Number
123	15.75 to N.wall 22.00 to E.wall	3rd Feb. 1905	

Sketch of Grave	Measurements	Bodies
	L: 1.00 m W: 0.80 m 1.0 below desert level	One

		Sex
		?

		Disturbed
	Special Notes	No

	Position
	Head north Face east

S.D. ?71-81

Stufen
IIIa2 -IIIb Protodynastic -Dynasty I

Pottery

Other Objects

Drawing	Type	Museum Number	Description	Museum Number
a			at X number of carnelian barrel beads + 2 bone bracelets one broken	
b	b.? L53j	LM.1972.319	under g - bone pin	
k	k.? W5la		under h was remnant of kohl wrapped in cloth	
c + d	under c crd ?L30p		around head were gr.gl. & carnelian beads	
f				
E	?L16b			
E oval in plan				
g+h				

Grave Number	Position in Cemetery	Date Excavated	Photograph Number
124	16.50 to N.wall 23.00 to E.wall	3rd. Feb. 1905	

Sketch of Grave

Measurements	Bodies
L: 1.85 m W: 1.00 m	One

	Sex
	?

Special Notes	Disturbed
	No

Position
Head north
Face east

S.D. ?52-80

Stufen
?IIIa1–IIIa2
Protodynastic

Pottery Drawing

Type	Museum Number	Other Objects Description	Museum Number
d ?L30p			
a ? R84			
b&c ?L36a			
f&g ?W51a			
h ?Proto.90u			

Grave Number	Position in Cemetery	Date Excavated	Photograph Number
125	14.00 to N.wall 20.00 to E.wall	3rd. Feb. 1905	

Sketch of Grave	Measurements	Bodies

Measurements

L: 1.00 m
W: 0.60 m

Bodies

One

Sex

?

Disturbed

No

Special Notes

Pelvis on its back also spine and ribs. Head on left side

Position
Head east
Face south

S.D.?70·77

Stufen
? IIIa2
Protodynastic

Pottery			Other Objects	
Drawing	Type	Museum Number	Description	Museum Number
b	? R24m		(a) palette	??LV.5346
c	? L25b	Bla. NN		

Grave Number	Position in Cemetery	Date Excavated	Photograph Number
126	11.00 to E.wall 27.00 to N.wall	4th Feb.1905	

Sketch of Grave	Measurements	Bodies

Measurements

L: 2.35m
W: 1.25m
D: 0.90m

Bodies
One

Sex
?

Disturbed
No

Special Notes

Lying on left side bones very decayed owing to wet sand. Legs crouched up and hands near face, legs covered by pottery.

Position
Head south

S.D.? 71-81

Stufen
IIIa2 - IIIb
Protodynastic - Dynasty I

Pottery

sand in all pots

Drawing	Type	Museum Number
a,b,c; ε,f,d	a? W51a	LM.16.11.05.138
g (broken)		
h	h? W62	
K L M; N P	?L36n	
R small dish over Q		

Q, R, S, T, V, W, X

S red clay ?W85
V+W ?W80
T x dark earth
Proto.Hbd8

Museum Number
T or X Bla.NN
V or W BM.42079

HIERAKONPOLIS FORT.　　GARSTANG EXCAVATION,1905.　GRAVE RECORD

Grave Number	Position in Cemetery	Date Excavated	Photograph Number
127	in redîm		

Sketch of Grave		Measurements	Bodies None
			Sex
			Disturbed
		Special Notes	Position
			S.D.
			Stufen

Pottery			Other Objects	
Drawing	Type	Museum Number	Description	Museum Number
6 dishes				

Grave Number	Position in Cemetery	Date Excavated	Photograph Number
128	28.00 to N. wall 9.00 to E. wall	4th Feb. 1905	

Sketch of Grave		Measurements	Bodies

	Measurements	Bodies
	L: 1.30 m W: 0.65 m	One
		Sex ?
		Disturbed No
	Special Notes Bones all broken	Position Head south Face west
		S.D. ?73-81
		Stufen IIIa2 = IIIb Protodynastic –

Pottery

Other Objects

Drawing	Type	Museum Number	Description	Museum Number
a +d h	c under d a. ?L30p		K piece of alabaster	
	?R24m			
	d full of black earth			
b	a + b full of sand ?L36n			
	g over f			
f	?R26a			

Grave Number	Position in Cemetery	Date Excavated	Photograph Number
129	8.00 to E.wall 27.20 to N.wall	4th Feb. 1905	

Sketch of Grave	Measurements	Bodies

	Measurements	Bodies
	L: 1.80m W. 1.75m	One
		Sex ?
		Disturbed Yes
	Special Notes Bones very broken	**Position** Head south Face west
		S.D. ?58-82
		Stufen ? IIIa1 -III b Protodynastic - Dynasty I

Pottery

Drawing	Type	Museum Number			Museum Number
a, f, b, g, K, l K full of black sand (charcoal powder)	?L30p		h	?L36n	
f					
c	? Proto.63e		M	?P24r	
Q P S	?W51a	Q,P or S Sh.J1905.94	N slate palette		LM.25.11.05.41
ε	E? R84	Sh.J.1905.96	shell under N		
R	?L53k		broken shell bracelet near head to W.		

Grave Number	Position in Cemetery	Date Excavated	Photograph Number
130	24.50 to N.Wall 8.00 to E.Wall	4th Feb. 1905	

Sketch of Grave		Measurements	Bodies

	Measurements	Bodies
	L: 1.70 m W: 0.90 m	One
		Sex ?
		Disturbed No
	Special Notes	Position Head south Face east
		S.D. ?71-81
		Stufen IIIa2-IIIb Protodynastic- Dynasty I

Pottery Drawing	Type	Museum Number	Other Objects Description	Museum Number
	?R24m		few carnelian and gr. glz. beads found above & under head arrangement uncertain	
	?R26a			
	?L36a			
	?L30p			
	?W51a			

a

f

ε   K under head

g   k

b

m l   d

n

c
h

Grave Number	Position in Cemetery	Date Excavated	Photograph Number
131	23.00 to E.Wall 14.25 to N.Wall	4th Feb.1905	

Sketch of Grave		Measurements	Bodies
		L: 1.40 m W: 0.90 m	One
			Sex ?
			Disturbed No
		Special Notes	
		Bones very decayed	**Position** Head east Face south
			S.D. ?58-61
			Stufen ?IIIa2-IIIb Protodynastic- Dynasty I

Pottery

Drawing	Type	Museum Number	**Other Objects** Description	Museum Number
 dish of rough pottery hand made				
 b full of dark sand & charcoal dust	?L36a			

HIERAKONPOLIS FORT.　　GARSTANG EXCAVATION,1905.　GRAVE RECORD

Grave Number	Position in Cemetery	Date Excavated	Photograph Number
132	12.50 to N.wall 14.75 to E.wall	4th Feb. 1905	

Sketch of Grave	Measurements	Bodies

	Measurements	Bodies
	L: 1.05m W: 0.60m	One
		Sex ?
		Disturbed No
	Special Notes Pelvis lying on its face, burial on its left side	**Position** Head south Face west
		S.D. ? 73-79
		Stufen ? IIa2 -IIIb Protodynastic- Dynasty I

Pottery			Other Objects	
Drawing	Type	Museum Number	Description	Museum Number
(a)	? R67			
c broken	L30p	LU.E6106		

Grave Number	Position in Cemetery	Date Excavated	Photograph Number
133	14.75 to N. wall 14.75 to E. wall	4th Feb. 1905	

Sketch of Grave	Measurements	Bodies
	L: 1.10 m W: 0.75m	One

		Sex
		?

		Disturbed
	Special Notes	No

		Position
		?

		S.D.? 73-80

		Stufen ? IIIa2 –IIIb Protodynastic- Dynasty I

Pottery

Drawing	Type	Museum Number
a, b,c + d — all very poor shape and broken a,b,c, +d full of dark powder + charcoal dust	? L30p	
g	? R24m	
L	? W51a	Sh.J1905.97
k	? L53k	

Other Objects

Description	Museum Number
at M black pebble N slate palette traces of green	

HIERAKONPOLIS FORT.   GARSTANG EXCAVATION,1905.   GRAVE RECORD

Grave Number	Position in Cemetery	Date Excavated	Photograph Number
134	16.75 from E.wall 16.00 from N wall	4th Feb.1905	

Sketch of Grave		Measurements	Bodies
		L: 0.90m W: 0.55 m	One
			Sex ?
			Disturbed No
		Special Notes	
			Position Head south Face west
			S.D.? 73-79
			Stufen ? IIIa2 - IIIb Protodynastic- Dynasty I

Pottery			Other Objects	
Drawing	Type	Museum Number	Description	Museum Number
b a inside b	? L30p			
fall of sand a	? W51a			
c d	? R24m			

Grave Number	Position in Cemetery	Date Excavated	Photograph Number
135	Redim between N.wall r outer wall	4th Feb. 1905	

Sketch of Grave	Measurements	Bodies
		None
		Sex
		Disturbed
	Special Notes	**Position**
		S.D. ? 73-79
		Stufen ?III a2 Protodynastic

Pottery

Drawing	Type	Museum Number	Other Objects Description	Museum Number
small dish			3 bracelets of shell, few beads	
	? W61			

Grave Number	Position in Cemetery	Date Excavated	Photograph Number
136	137 / passage / 136 / S.E. corner of fort	4th. Feb. 1905	

Sketch of Grave	Measurements	Bodies
	L: 0.70 m W: 0.65 m	One

		Sex
		Infant

		Disturbed
	Special Notes	Yes
	Broken bones	

		Position
		Head east Face north

		S.D. ?46-68

		Stufen
		?IId1 -IId2 Gerzean

Pottery				Other Objects	
Drawing		Type	Museum Number	Description	Museum Number
a	decorated with wave pattern	D10K	LU.E6099	ε	LU.E5359
b		?P84i			
c	dark red glaze	PR93a	LU.E4434		
d		?R38			

Grave Number	Position in Cemetery	Date Excavated	Photograph Number
137		4th Feb. 1905	

Sketch of Grave

	Measurements	Bodies
	L: 1.60m W: 1.00m	One

Sex
?

Disturbed
No

Special Notes	Position
2 green pebbles in front of face	Head west Face north

S.D. ?47-76

Stufen
?IIc -IId2 Gerzean

Pottery

Drawing	Type	Museum Number		Museum Number
a dark earth inside	?R84d		d inserted and used as cover for E	
g			L used as cover for P	
b dark clay broken L	b.?R76h		?R81	
H	?D7c	?S.W. W104b	?R84e	
k			x bone vessel	
c	c.?R84		slate palette ?148	
N	?D61k			

Grave Number	Position in Cemetery	Date Excavated	Photograph Number
138	2.70 to N.wall 1.70 to W.wall	5th Feb.1905	H.29

Sketch of Grave	Measurements	Bodies
	L: 1.50m	One

0.80　　0.75

Measurements

L: 1.50m

W: 0.80m + 0.75m

D: 1.50m

	Bodies
	One
	Sex
	?
	Disturbed

Special Notes

Pit.
Burial lying on left side
pelvis on its back,
right hand to face and
inside right arm at X
shell bracelets + beads
Under (a) was brown
pebble burnished

Disturbed
No
Position
Face east
Head south
S.D. ?75-79
Stufen
IIIa2-IIIb
Protodynastic- Dynasty I

Pottery

Drawing

a

Type	Museum Number
? Proto 16d	
?W62 Painted Cylinder f or g	Ot. Exchange from LM. (25.11.05.2)

Other Objects

Description

Beads found near X
used apparently as
a bracelet as the
left arm was through
the stringing
9 bracelets in all
found

dark   light   dark
stone   ones   stone
beads | beads
        1 light green

c
3 ins   Small slate palette

b   small alabaster vase
        2 ins

Museum Number

one LM. 13.12.05.45
three LM. 25.11.05.45
a,b,c.

HIERAKONPOLIS FORT.   GARSTANG EXCAVATION,1905.   GRAVE RECORD

Grave Number	Position in Cemetery	Date Excavated	Photograph Number
139	3.60 m to W. wall 1.55 m to N. wall	5th Feb. 1905	

Sketch of Grave	Measurements	Bodies

	Measurements	**Bodies**
	L: 1.50m	One
	W: 0.80m + 0.80m	**Sex**
	D: 1.50m	?
		Disturbed
	Special Notes	No
	Lying on left side with left arm on hip	**Position** Head south Face west
		S.D. ? 78-79
		Stufen ? III a 2 – III b Protodynastic – Dynasty I

Pottery

Drawing	Type	Museum Number	Other Objects Description	Museum Number
a	? R26f			
b and c	? Proto. 46F6	AMS. E15670 (on loan to NMS)		
	Proto. 46k	WAS. A229		

Grave Number	Position in Cemetery	Date Excavated	Photograph Number
140	3.40 to W.wall 5.25 to N.wall	5th. Feb.1905	H.79, H.81

Sketch of Grave	Measurements	Bodies
	L: 2.15 m W: 0.80m D: 0.30m below desert level	Two

	Measurements	Sex
		Male +?

	Special Notes	Disturbed
	Burial bricked around to keep out sand	Yes

		Position
		Heads once South

		S.D. ? 78-80

		Stufen
		? III b Dynasty I

Pottery

Drawing		Type	Museum Number			Museum Number
a	E f g h	? R24m		L M	? L36a	
c	h inside k	? R2bc	Car. 75.773			
		c ? W90				
d	N Q V	d.? L36a			T piece of alabaster vessel	LM.1973.1.697
		N Q V ? Proto. 50q			b on either side of b burnished pebbles	LU.E5308a
	R like above but decorated	? Proto.49L				LU.E5308b
	O,M,P	? R2ba				
s		? L57k				

Grave Number	Position in Cemetery	Date Excavated	Photograph Number
141	⊓.25 to W. wall 5.00 to N. wall		H.82

Sketch of Grave	Measurements	Bodies
		One

	Measurements	
	L: 2.40m W: 0.80m	**Sex** ?
		Disturbed Yes
	Special Notes	**Position** Once head South
		S.D.? ⊓⊓-80
		Stufen ?[Ⅲa2]-Ⅲb Dynasty Ⅰ

Pottery

Drawing	Type	Museum Number		Museum Number
small dish as cover	L36b	a,c or m WAS.A225	L red pottery Proto. 46F6	LU.E6863
E		Bowl LM 13.12.05.8 missing		
a c M	f			
V	? R26a		M ? R27	
b r d	b+d ? Proto.63e		t L⊓1G	
K				
R under R another similar				
N O P Q S	?W85			

HIERAKONPOLIS FORT.   GARSTANG EXCAVATION,1905.   GRAVE RECORD

Grave Number	Position in Cemetery	Date Excavated	Photograph Number
142	9.75 to W.Wall 5.10 to N.wall	5th Feb. 1905	H.83

Sketch of Grave	Measurements	Bodies
	L: 1.70m W: 1.00m	One

		Sex
		?

		Disturbed
	Special Notes	Yes
	in h brown pebble	Position
		Once head south
		S.D.? 75-81
		Stufen ? IIIa2 -IIIb Protodynastic - Dynasty I

Pottery

Drawing	Type	Museum Number		Museum Number
a	? Proto 63j		d light pottery	
m	? R24m		? Proto 63e	
R g N			ε	? W62 K L
Q	? R70		? L36a	
h	? R26a			
c light pottery P	? L59c		s slate palette	Ob. Exchanged with LM, 1913 (LM.13.12.05.11)

Grave Number	Position in Cemetery	Date Excavated	Photograph Number
143		6th Feb. 1905	

Sketch of Grave	Measurements	Bodies
	L: 2.70 m W: 1.40 m	?

		Sex
		?

		Disturbed

Special Notes

N. end of burial under outer wall Outside N. wall.
S end of tomb touching wall

Position

S.D. ? 73-80

Stufen
? IIIa2-IIIb Protodynastic - Dynasty I

Pottery

Drawing	Type	Museum Number		Museum Number
a	? R2ba		k ? L16c	
c RT V UX rW	? L30p	AMS.E15675 (CMU1461)	d r s ? Wb2 Pr Q ? Proto.81f	d or S Sh.J1905.88
	? L30s		h	
under d ε like	? R2ba	RISW.AX.121.12	W ? L36L	
n under g k l m n			f slate palette	
g				

HIERAKONPOLIS FORT.   GARSTANG EXCAVATION,1905.   GRAVE RECORD

Grave Number	Position in Cemetery	Date Excavated	Photograph Number
144		5th Feb.1905	

Sketch of Grave			Measurements	Bodies
				none
				Sex
				Disturbed
			Special Notes	
			in redim	Position
				S.D. ?75-80
				Stufen
				? IIIa2 -IIIb
				Protodynastic - Dynasty I

Pottery			Other Objects	
Drawing	Type	Museum Number	Description	Museum Number
	? L36a			
	Proto. 50G	Cat. 75.770		
	? W62			

Grave Number	Position in Cemetery	Date Excavated	Photograph Number
145	12.00 to W. wall north side under N. wall	6th. Feb. 1905	

Sketch of Grave ↓	Measurements	Bodies

Measurements

L: 1.65 m

W: 1.90 m

Special Notes

Two burials are on either side of pit female to left, burial to right lying on its face with legs bent up, no remains of head

Bodies
Two

Sex
Female
Male

Disturbed
Yes

Position
Heads north and south

S.D. ?71-82

Stufen
?IIIa2 -IIIb
Protodynastic -
Dynasty I

Pottery

Drawing	Type	Museum Number		Museum Number

a ? Proto. 63e

b + c Proto. 65u   LV. E6091

? W61

d ? R26f

f ? L19c

g

A r c — red glaze ? P4bk

B ?W51

D ?L59 d

slate palette under f

E alabaster vase

Grave Number	Position in Cemetery	Date Excavated	Photograph Number
146	2.45 to W. corner	6th Feb. 1905	H.84

Sketch of Grave	Measurements	Bodies
line of N. wall	L: 1.90 m W: 0.80 m	One
		Sex ?
		Disturbed Yes
	Special Notes Much disturbed bones all displaced pit cut into hard encrusted gebel-like Sabbach	Position Head once north
		S.D.? 78-80
		Stufen ? IIIb Dynasty I

Pottery

Drawing	Type	Museum Number
a / + b		
E	Proto 70m	
L piece of broken dish, fine clay		
f h k yellow surface	? W80	RISW.AX121.7
g	? Proto.95R	

Other Objects

Description	Museum Number
c broken alabaster cf. H19	LU.E2516x
d slate palette broken	LM.13.12.06.12
near d was stone pebble	

Grave Number	Position in Cemetery	Date Excavated	Photograph Number
147	180 to N. wall 500 to W. wall	6th. Feb. 1905	

Sketch of Grave		Measurements	Bodies
		L: 2.10m W: 1.00m D: 1.00m	One

	Measurements	Sex
		?

	Disturbed
	Yes

Special Notes	Position
Bones displaced	Head once south

	S.D. ?75-82

	Stufen
	?IIIa2 -IIIb Protodynastic- Dynasty I

Pottery

Drawing	Type	Museum Number
a+d E small dish like a		
c under E another pot like b	? R26f	
b g like b	? W62	painted vase LM.16.11.0640 missing
g		
f M r N	? L36b	M or N Bol.44.05.14

Other Objects

Description	Museum Number
K † L ? Proto.63e	K or L Bla. NN.

HIERAKONPOLIS FORT.   GARSTANG EXCAVATION,1905.   GRAVE RECORD

Grave Number	Position in Cemetery	Date Excavated	Photograph Number
147B	3.25 from N. corner South under the wall	6th Feb. 1905	

Sketch of Grave	Measurements	Bodies
	50 m deep L: 1.30 m	none

		Sex

		Disturbed

	Special Notes	Position
	Nothing found in it possibly because wall was on level of desert in which tomb was cut.	

		S.D.

		Stufen

Pottery			Other Objects	
Drawing	Type	Museum Number	Description	Museum Number

Grave Number	Position in Cemetery	Date Excavated	Photograph Number
149	20.00 to W.wall 2.00 to N.wall	6th Feb. 1905	

Sketch of Grave	Measurements	Bodies
	L: 1.50m W: 0.80m	One

	Measurements	
		Sex ?
		Disturbed No
	Special Notes	**Position** Head south Face west
		S.D.? 77-81
		Stufen ? IIIa 2-IIIb Protodynastic- Dynasty I

Pottery

Drawing	Type	Museum Number
a,E	?R24m	
b	L36n	RISW.AX:121.4.
d	?L12d	
f+g	Proto. 46F6	Bol.44.05.7 LU.E6861 painted pot LH.13.12.05.1 missing

Other Objects

Description	Museum Number
c Slate palette	LU.E5340

Grave Number	Position in Cemetery	Date Excavated	Photograph Number
148	23.00 to N.wall 12.75 to E.wall	6th Feb.1905	

Sketch of Grave	Measurements	Bodies

legs apparently here

Measurements

L: 1.50m

W: 1.60m

Bodies
One

Sex
?

Disturbed
No

Special Notes

No bones found in position all decayed through damp
Near 148 to E black topped vase red glaze

Position
Head once South

S.D.?71-75

Stufen
?IIIa2-IIIb
Protodynastic -
Dynasty I

Pottery

Drawing	Type	Museum Number		Museum Number
a	?Proto.73s (no neck)		f	
d	?W90		c	?Proto.60k
			?W51a	
g h k	?Proto.44bd		E ?Proto.87g	
b r Q	?.Proto.60j		M ?Proto. 2d	
L	?R24m		P broken ?Proto 73	
			+ ?Proto. 86F2	
			S slate palette	

Grave Number	Position in Cemetery	Date Excavated	Photograph Number
150	9.50 to E.wall 5.00 to N.wall	8th Feb. 1905	

Sketch of Grave		Measurements	Bodies

Measurements

L: 1.00m
W: 0.68m
D: 0.50m
Below desert level

Special Notes

Burial lying on its face, much decayed
Legs doubled up as though the burial kneeling

Bodies
One

Sex
?

Disturbed
No

Position
Head south
Face west

S.D. ?73-79

Stufen
? IIIa2 - IIIb
Protodynastic-
Dynasty I

Pottery

Drawing	Type	Museum Number
a	? Proto. 87e	
b (broken mouth)	? L4b	
c r f	? L30p	
d		
E	? R24m	

Other Objects

Description	Museum Number
X slate palette apparently encased in "boase"	LM.13.12.05.13

Green glazed beads and a few carnelian found under and over head.

Large carnelian beads and large pendant found round neck

Kohl and brown pebble found under right hand.

Grave Number	Position in Cemetery	Date Excavated	Photograph Number
151	2.00 to N. wall 25.00 to E. wall	8th Feb.1905	

Sketch of Grave		Measurements	Bodies

			One
		L: 1.10 m	
		W: 0.75 m	Sex
		D: 0.85 m	?
			Disturbed
		Special Notes	No
		Burial in Sabbach	Position
			?
			S.D.? 75-81
			Stufen
			IIIa2 - IIIb Protodynastic-Dynasty I

Pottery			Other Objects	
Drawing	Type	Museum Number	Description	Museum Number

a	L36a	LU.E4890		
b, c	? Proto 4b or W 62	Sh.J.1905.95		

Grave Number	Position in Cemetery	Date Excavated	Photograph Number
152		8th Feb. 1905	

Sketch of Grave	Measurements	Bodies None
		Sex
		Disturbed
	Special Notes	Position
		S.D. ?77-81
		Stufen ?IIIa2 -IIIb Protodynastic-Dynasty I

Pottery

Drawing	Type	Museum Number	Other Objects Description	Museum Number
b	L17m	WAM. A231	a — slate palette	
d mishapen + ptmk 11/		BM.42096	brown pebble in b	
c	?R24m			

Grave Number	Position in Cemetery	Date Excavated	Photograph Number
153	11.00 to E. wall 11.00 to N. wall	8th Feb. 1905	

Sketch of Grave		Measurements	Bodies

Measurements

L: 0.90m

W: 0.50m

⚓

Bodies	One
Sex	?
Disturbed	No

Special Notes

Lying on right side with arms in front of face, burial on surface of old desert level

Brick at head .13 × .28 × .8

Position	Head south. Face west
S.D. ?	77-82
Stufen	? III b Protodynastic – Dynasty I

Pottery

Drawing	Type	Museum Number	Other Objects Description	Museum Number
a	? L 59G			
b	? Proto. 63e			
c	P 81 b	Car. 75.771		

Grave Number	Position in Cemetery	Date Excavated	Photograph Number
154	11.00 to E. wall 13.00 to N. wall	8th Feb. 1905	

Sketch of Grave	Measurements	Bodies
	L: 0.75 W: 0.45 Burial on desert level	One

Measurements

L: 0.75

W: 0.45

Burial on desert level

Sex	?
Special Notes	**Disturbed** No
Remnants of "ginzana" in front of face	**Position** Head south Face west
	S.D. ? 73-80
	Stufen ? IIIa2 - IIIb Protodynastic - Dynasty I

Pottery

Drawing	Type	Museum Number	Other Objects — Description	Museum Number
a	? L30p		slate palette traces of green	L.U. E5304
b	L59d	AMS. E15673	bone pendant r few carnelian beads found around neck	
c	R65b	BM. 42097		
ε f & g	? R24m			

Grave Number	Position in Cemetery	Date Excavated	Photograph Number
155	10.00 to E. wall 13.00 to N. wall	8th Feb. 1905	

Sketch of Grave	Measurements	Bodies

Measurements

L: 0.85m

W: 0.60m

Apparently 0.20m above old desert level

Special Notes

Lying on right side.

Bodies
One

Sex
?

Disturbed
No

Position
Head east
Face north

S.D. ?56-80

Stufen
? IIIa1-IIIb
Protodynastic

Pottery

Drawing

Type	Museum Number
? L17n	
? L53k	

Other Objects

Description

c brown pebble
d shell with small flints
e dom fruit

Museum Number

HIERAKONPOLIS FORT.   GARSTANG EXCAVATION,1905.   GRAVE RECORD

Grave Number	Position in Cemetery	Date Excavated	Photograph Number
156	11.00 to E.wall 14.00 to N.wall	8th Feb. 1905	

Sketch of Grave	Measurements	Bodies

Measurements

L: 1.00m

W: 0.75m

Special Notes

Bodies	One
Sex	?
Disturbed	No
Position	Head west Face north
S.D.	?73-81
Stufen	? IIIa2 - IIIb Probody nastic - Dynasty I

Pottery

Other Objects

Drawing	Type	Museum Number	Description	Museum Number
a ε h k n p	?R24m			
c	?L36n			
m	?R45a			
b d L full of dark earth	?L30p			
f g	?W51a			

Grave Number	Position in Cemetery	Date Excavated	Photograph Number
157	12.50 to N.wall 4.50 to E. wall		

Sketch of Grave	Measurements	Bodies
	L: 1.30m	One
	W. 1.00m	Sex
	D: 1.00m below old desert level	?
		Disturbed
	Special Notes	? Yes
	Bones very broken and head smashed legs stuck up in air and apart and lying on back. Traces of mud covering 0.40m below old desert level	Position
		Head south-east
		S.D. ?70-79
		Stufen
		?IIIa1-IIIb Protodynastic - Dynasty I

Pottery

Drawing	Type	Museum Number
a b	? Proto. 60k	
		Painted vase cf. D20q RISW. AX121.8
c d	R57e	BM.42093
f g h	? Proto.46 D2	g or h V+A.593.1905

Other Objects

Description	Museum Number
rough pieces of slate palette.	

Grave Number	Position in Cemetery	Date Excavated	Photograph Number
158	1.80 from E.wall 34.50 from N.wall	10th Feb. 1905	

Sketch of Grave	Measurements	Bodies

	Measurements	Bodies
	L: 1.30 m W: 0.85 m D: 1.00 m	One
		Sex ?
		Disturbed No
	Special Notes	**Position** Head south Face west
		S.D. ? 60-73
		Stufen ? IId2 -IIIa1 Late Gerzean -Protodynastic

Pottery			Other Objects	
Drawing	Type	Museum Number	Description	Museum Number

Pottery drawings:
- a
- b — Small pot poor clay
- c — decorated with red stripes — ? D20m — LM.25.11.05.19 missing
- d — ? R65c — d or E Bla.NN
- ε
- broken g — ? R38

Other Objects:
- f — Slate palette
- 2 brown pebbles under palette
- Copper bracelet on right arm
- Beads found under and over head, pendants etc
- broken hair pin at X

HIERAKONPOLIS FORT.   GARSTANG EXCAVATION,1905.   GRAVE RECORD

Grave Number	Position in Cemetery	Date Excavated	Photograph Number
159	10.50 to E.wall 19.00 to N.wall	10th Feb. 1905	

Sketch of Grave		Measurements	Bodies
		L: 1.15 m	One
		W: 0.50m	**Sex** ?
		D: 0.80m below gebel	**Disturbed** No
		Special Notes	**Position** Head south Face west
			S.D.? 70-77
			Stufen ? IIIa2 Protodynastic

Pottery				Other Objects	
Drawing	Type	Museum Number		Description	Museum Number
a poor shape					
b c under b+c small dish	? R24m				
d	? R38				

Grave Number	Position in Cemetery	Date Excavated	Photograph Number
160	10.50 to E.wall 19.00 to N.wall	10th Feb. 1905	

Sketch of Grave	Measurements	Bodies
	L: 2.00 m W: 1.00 m D: 1.10 m	One

Measurements

L: 2.00 m
W: 1.00 m
D: 1.10 m

Special Notes

Bodies
One

Sex
?

Disturbed
No

Position
Head west
Face north

S.D. ?63-79

Stufen
?IIIa1-IIIb
Protodynastic

Pottery

Drawing	Type	Museum Number		Museum Number

Type

?L30p

?W43b
or W51a

?P97m

R.? B39a
bg. ?L17n

?R26f

black top
fine bowl
red inside black out

M

N
red glaze   ?P4ba

?Proto 60j

slate palette

Carnelian beads on head.

HIERAKONPOLIS FORT. GARSTANG EXCAVATION, 1905. GRAVE RECORD

Grave Number	Position in Cemetery	Date Excavated	Photograph Number
161	9.00 to E. wall 16.50 to N. wall	10th Feb. 1905	

Sketch of Grave		Measurements	Bodies

Measurements
L: 1.20 m
W: 0.60 m

Special Notes
Head on left side, body lying on back

Bodies: One
Sex: ?
Disturbed: No
Position
Head south
Face west
S.D. ? 77-79
Stufen
? IIIa2 IIIb
Protodynastic Dynasty I

Pottery

Drawing	Type	Museum Number
a, b	? Proto. 60j	
c	? Proto. 46D³	
K	? L19p	

Other Objects

Description	Museum Number
d shell	
five brown pebbles (f to E)	
e portion of alabaster bowl	
f slate palette	
g oyster shell	LW. E3302

Grave Number	Position in Cemetery	Date Excavated	Photograph Number
162		10th Feb.1905	

Sketch of Grave	Measurements	Bodies
	L: 0.80m W: 0.60m	None
		Sex
		Disturbed
	Special Notes No bones found	**Position**
		S.D.?71–79
		Stufen ?IIIa2-IIIb Predynastic – Dynasty I

Pottery

Other Objects

Drawing	Type	Museum Number	Description	Museum Number
a	?L30p		under d were brown pebble	
b	?W51a		bone copper r pieces of copper sulphate	
c	?L42			
d rε	?R24m			

Grave Number	Position in Cemetery	Date Excavated	Photograph Number
163	3.00 to E.wall 14.75 to N.wall	10th Feb.1905	

Sketch of Grave		Measurements	Bodies
		L: 0.60m	One
		W: 0.40m	Sex
			Infant
			Disturbed
		Special Notes	No
		Infant burial	Position Head east Face south
			S.D. ?73-76
			Stufen ?IIIa2 Protodynastic

Pottery

Drawing	Type	Museum Number	Other Objects Description	Museum Number
a	?P4ba	Wavy-handled vase Glu:23.3%	c thick slate + brown pebble over	
b				?Flint LU.E6638

HIERAKONPOLIS FORT.   GARSTANG EXCAVATION,1905.   GRAVE RECORD

Grave Number	Position in Cemetery	Date Excavated	Photograph Number
164	4.25 to E.wall 15.00 to N.wall	10th Feb.1905	

Sketch of Grave		Measurements	Bodies

Measurements

L: 1.20m

W: 0.70m

Bodies

One

Sex

?

Disturbed

No

Special Notes

Position

Head south
Face west

S.D.? 78-79

Stufen

? IIIa2 - IIIb
Protodynastic
— Dynasty I

Pottery

Drawing

a

b

d had small dish as cover

d

Type	Museum Number
? Proto 60j	
? R2ba	
? L36a	

Other Objects

Description

c   slate palette

Museum Number

HIERAKONPOLIS FORT.   GARSTANG EXCAVATION,1905.   GRAVE RECORD

Grave Number	Position in Cemetery	Date Excavated	Photograph Number
165	17.30 to N.wall 5.50 to E.wall	10th Feb. 1905	

Sketch of Grave	Measurements	Bodies
	L: 1.25m W: 0.80m	One

Measurements

L: 1.25m

W: 0.80m

Bodies One

Sex ?

Disturbed No

Special Notes

Pelvis on its back

Position
Head south-east
Face west

S.D. ?56-78

Stufen
?IIIa1 - IIIa2
Protodynastic

Pottery			Other Objects	
Drawing	Type	Museum Number	Description	Museum Number
a	? L17n			
b + c	? R24m			

HIERAKONPOLIS FORT.   GARSTANG EXCAVATION,1905.   GRAVE RECORD

Grave Number	Position in Cemetery	Date Excavated	Photograph Number
166	7.25 to E.wall 18.50 to N.wall	10th Feb.1905	

Sketch of Grave	Measurements	Bodies

	L: 0.90m W. 0.75 m	**Bodies** One
		Sex ?
		Disturbed No
	Special Notes Burial lying on back with legs up	**Position** Head south
		S.D.?77-78
		Stufen ?IIIa2-IIIb Protodynastic-Dynasty I

Pottery Drawing	Type	Museum Number	Other Objects Description	Museum Number
a			slate palette	
b	?L36n			

HIERAKONPOLIS FORT.   GARSTANG EXCAVATION,1905.   GRAVE RECORD

Grave Number	Position in Cemetery	Date Excavated	Photograph Number
167	28.00 to N. wall 6.50 to E. wall	11th Feb. 1905	

Sketch of Grave	Measurements	Bodies
	L. 1.30 m N. 0.90m D: 1.30 m	One
		Sex ?
		Disturbed No
	Special Notes Bones very damaged but traces remaining	**Position** Head north Face east
		S.D.? 73-79
		Stufen ? IIIa 2 Protodynastic

Pottery			Other Objects	
Drawing	**Type**	**Museum Number**	**Description**	**Museum Number**
a r E — below a another similar but smaller e full of dark sand + charcoal dust	? Proto.60g		c slate palette under c was brown pebble	
b r f	? W61	b or f Sh.J1905.89		
dish under E	? R24m			
d	? L42			

Grave Number	Position in Cemetery	Date Excavated	Photograph Number
168	6.00 to E.wall 31.50 to N.wall	11th Feb. 1905	

Sketch of Grave	Measurements	Bodies
	L: 1.30m W: 1.20m D: 1.50m	One

Measurements

L: 1.30m

W: 1.20m

D: 1.50m

Bodies — One

Sex — ?

Disturbed — No

Special Notes

Burial lying on face

Position

Head south
Face west

S.D. ?56-78

Stufen

?IId2 - IIIa1
Late Gerzean
- Protodynastic

Pottery

Drawing	Type	Museum Number
M a c g +h	? L30p	
b j	? R24m	
d red glaze	? P93b	
E	L17n	WAM A232
k	L17m	BM.42133
o,P	P1c	LU.E4593
N red glaze black inside		LM.25.11.05.25 missing

Other Objects

Description	Museum Number
f red glaze P97k	LU.E6086
L ? R45a	
few green glazed beads found under head.	

Grave Number	Position in Cemetery	Date Excavated	Photograph Number
169	4.00 to E.wall 7.50 to N.wall	11th Feb. 1905	

Sketch of Grave	Measurements	Bodies

Measurements

L: 1.55m

W: 1.20m

Special Notes

Bodies
One

Sex
?

Disturbed
No

Position
Head south
Face west

S.D.? 75-79

Stufen
? IIIa2-IIIb
Protodynastic-
Dynasty I

Pottery			Other Objects	
Drawing	Type	Museum Number	Description	Museum Number

Drawing

a
b
c
d e
f
g h
k
L

Coated with mud

Type

? R24m

? R2ba

? L17n
? W62

? Prota.63j

? Proto.60k

Grave Number	Position in Cemetery	Date Excavated	Photograph Number
170	18.50 to W.wall 2.00 to N.wall	11th Feb. 1905	

Sketch of Grave	Measurements	Bodies
	L: 1.20m W: 0.75m	One

Measurements	Bodies
	Sex ?
	Disturbed ?
Special Notes	Position ?
Burial in sabbach	S.D.? 77
	Stufen ? IIIa2 Protodynastic

Pottery			Other Objects	
Drawing	Type	Museum Number	Description	Museum Number
	? Proto.63j			

HIERAKONPOLIS FORT.   GARSTANG EXCAVATION,1905.   GRAVE RECORD

Grave Number	Position in Cemetery	Date Excavated	Photograph Number
171 ₊ 172	Burials in W. wall (171 - N)		H.85

Sketch of Grave			Measurements	Bodies Two
				Sex ?
				Disturbed No
			Special Notes	
				Position Extended
				S.D.
				Stufen Dynastic

Pottery			Other Objects	
Drawing	Type	Museum Number	Description	Museum Number

Analysis

The preceding grave record sheets present the details
from Garstang's notebooks i) and ii) for 166 of the 188
graves which he excavated beneath the Fort in 1905. As
stated in the preface, I made written contact with all
the museums in the places on Garstang's manuscript
distribution list (see Appendix C) to locate the present
whereabouts of the objects from the excavation, and,
considering the time that has elapsed, received a very
favourable response. Some museums generously supplied
photographs which provided an aid to the identification
of the pottery corpus types (Petrie, 1921, 1923). These
were chiefly assigned from a careful study of Garstang's
photographs and drawings, and personal study of the
objects in the following museums: School of Archaeology
and Oriental Studies, University of Liverpool; National
Museums and Galleries on Merseyside, Liverpool (about a
third of the objects were lost during the Second World
War); Central Museum and Art Gallery, Bolton; Townley
Hall Museum, Burnley; Wellcome Museum, University
College Swansea and the British Museum, London.
Obviously, only those pots which I have handled, or for
which good modern photographs are available, can be
typed with any certainty, and I have been careful to
insert a question mark for all the identifications of
which I cannot be sure. Fortunately, most of the
material from the excavation was kept in the two museums
in Liverpool. Where no excavation photographs exist,
typing from the inadequate unscaled sketches is extremely
risky and in some cases I have not attempted it. A
subtle change in the curve of the body of a pot, or the
way in which its rim arises from the neck, can signify a
different type and therefore the possibility of another
date for the assemblage.

After I had located all the objects that seemed possible at this stage (see Preface), I carefully assigned corpus numbers to the pottery using Petrie's typology, but not applying the refinements now possible in Federn's revision, which would have been useful, particularly to divide the L ware into his S (smooth), P1 (smooth with polished red finish) and P2 (half polished bowls) groups (Needler, 1981), as it would not have been entirely feasible because of the paucity of descriptive information on the wares with Garstang's black and white photographs and sketches. I then attempted to date the graves. I did this by first assigning a Sequence Date, according to Petrie's system, and then a Stufen number (Kaiser, 1957). All uncertainties are again indicated by a question mark. The results for all the recorded graves confirmed Kemp's dating (Kemp, 1963) of the material in the University of Liverpool's collection: the bulk were Naqada II to Naqada III/early Dynasty I. There were eleven intrusive Dynastic, post Archaic, graves and thirteen find spots which were not graves. The map which Kemp prepared from Garstang's sketch map (Document I, see Appendix A) and his plottings in the notebook entries (Kemp, 1963) were checked, and one or two graves were added. The map was then re-drawn with shading added to indicate the dates of the graves (see end section).

It can be seen clearly on the new map that there was a geographical shift in the use of the cemetery during the late Predynastic, which accords with Hoffman's surface survey. The earlier graves (Naqada II) are chiefly located to the east of the Fort near and under the entrance, and as time progressed the cemetery spread to the west; graves transitional between Naqada II and III were located north of the centre of the Fort, and then on to the west, where the early Dynasty I graves were situated. This seems to accord with the results of the Metropolitan Museum's excavation of 1934 (Lansing, 1935), which cleared one hundred graves outside the entrance of the Fort and into the Great Wadi on the south-east side. Logan (personal communication) has said that the date for most of the pottery from these graves is Naqada II with a relative abundance of painted (D) wares, although some of the pottery now on display in the Metropolitan Museum from this excavation includes types known in Naqada III. Surface surveys of the area north, east and west (behind) the Fort by Hoffman and others in recent years have indicated that the cemetery extended well beyond the walls, and there is also a late Predynastic settlement area (Locality 27A, see topographic map in Hoffman *et al*, 1982) within it, that was finally overrun by the cemetery as it grew to the west.

A glance at this large scale map in the Egyptian Studies

Association's first report will also indicate the prox-
imity of this "Fort" cemetery to the town site of
Nekhen and its distance from the Gerzean cemetery,
Locality Hk-33, in which Green found the famous painted
tomb 100 (Quibell and Green, 1900; Case and Payne, 1962;
Kemp, 1973; Adams, 1974b). It would be tempting to
identify the Fort cemetery as the main burial place used
by the inhabitants of Nekhen during the late Predynastic
and Protodynastic-Dynasty I periods, when this town was
the capital of Upper Egypt. There is, however, another
contender for the cemetery of the ruling classes of
Nekhen at this time at Locality 6, twenty-five kilo-
metres up the Great Wadi (Wadi Abul Suffian). Since the
excavations there in 1979-80 (Hoffman et al, 1982), which
uncovered two large tombs numbered 1 and 2, further work
in 1982 produced two more large graves (tombs 10 and 11)
near tomb 1 (Hoffman, 1983). Of these, Tomb 11, although
thoroughly looted, produced traces of worked ivory;
lapis lazuli flies and shells; obsidian and crystal
blades; carnelian, garnet, turquoise, faience, gold and
silver beads; a carved wooden bed with bulls' feet, and
the usual abundance of pottery sherds, including painted
types of the Protodynastic period. As the graves that
Garstang dug were in the main undisturbed, and there
were no graves of comparable size and none with items
of such an exotic nature, it seems safe at this point
to venture the opinion that the Fort cemetery served
for the bulk of the town's population during the later
Predynastic and Early Dynastic periods, whilst the
cemetery in the wadi, which had also been important
during the middle Predynastic, Naqada I-II (Adams, 1982),
was for the interment of the local elite. Further
excavations are planned at the so-called Gerzean cemetery (Hk-33) to the south-east on the edge of the cultivation, and these should be able to reveal if there was
an area within this cemetery during the middle Predynastic which contained the richer graves like cemetery T at Naqada (fifty-five percent of which had ten
or more objects); a possibility suggested by the pres-
ence of the painted tomb and at least four other large
rectangular graves (Adams, 1974b). Of course, further
excavations behind the Fort would not only elucidate
this present reconstructed record, but might also
complicate the issue by revealing wealthy graves of the
Protodynastic and Early Dynastic periods; perhaps the
raison d'être for the building of the mud brick Fort.
The larger rectangular graves in Garstang's cemetery
were mainly clustered in the north-west corner of the
Fort, and an incised pottery coffin lid of early Dynasty
I was found in a looted grave just west of the Fort in
1980 (Hoffman et al, 1982, pp.35-38).

An interesting parallel is provided by a disturbed
Predynastic cemetery recently excavated at El Kab with-

in the Dynastic town enclosure (Hendrickx, 1984). It
yielded one hundred graves which date, like this
cemetery, to Naqada III/Dynasty I. One group of the
latest graves there was characterized by reinforcement
with large sandstone slabs and separation of the grave
goods from the deceased. Other than this fashion, in
the burial of old male adults, the style and content of
the interments across the river Nile, with larger stor-
age jars around the feet and smaller pots and objects
near the chest and head, were very similar to those in
the Hierakonpolis Fort cemetery. The exotic items
(stone vessels, beads, palettes, bracelets, spoons, hair-
pins) seem more numerous, although this was a plundered
cemetery, which would seem to indicate that it repres-
ented a mixed society with stratified classes rather
than the postulated separation of the upper class to
another cemetery as at Hierakonpolis (for clustering of
large and rich graves in other Predynastic cemeteries
see Castillos, 1983). So far, other than scattered
surface sherds, there is little to indicate Predynastic
settlement at El Kab (Nekheb), later a twin city to
Hierakonpolis (Nekhen) which took precedence in the
Middle and New Kingdoms although, as at Hierakonpolis,
there may be traces of occupation below the alluvium.

In any case, this report should virtually complete the
record (see Chapter 1, note 1) of past excavation at
Hierakonpolis by British Egyptologists and add to the
data on the Predynastic cemeteries there, which have
been so poorly served in print. The famous royal and
votive artifacts excavated last century in the city of
Nekhen (Quibell and Green, 1900, 1902; Adams, 1974),
the mass of material from the settlement sites
(Hoffman *et al*, 1982) and the revelation (by coring)
in 1984 that there was substantial (3.5 m) Predynastic
settlement under Nekhen (Hoffman, 1986; Hoffman,
Hamroush and Allen, *forthcoming*) would all seem to
confirm Hierakonpolis as the late Predynastic capital
of Upper Egypt, as recorded in legend. Naqada, however,
was championed as the capital by Elise Baumgartel
(Baumgartel, 1970) because of the size and richness of
the cemeteries, and Fekri Hassan's recent work there has
also revealed further settlement sites of middle and
late Predynastic date with earlier C14 dates than those
at Hierakonpolis, but covering a surprisingly small
area. Hassan (personal communication) now feels that
many of the settlements were destroyed. It seems that
the floruit of the Naqada II (Gerzean) culture was at
Naqada, its influence spreading south to Hierakonpolis,
which then became more important in the last phase of
prehistory (Kemp, 1977). As the focus of the region it
became the repository for heraldic representations of
the unification, which does not seem in fact to have
been historical fact presaged by the bloody battles of

legend (Wildung, 1984; Kroeper, 1985), but rather the
result of country-wide evolution from Predynastic
expansion and consolidation into a nation state.

When the typing of the material and the dating of the
graves here was complete, Theya Molleson, from the Sub-
Department of Anthropology at the British Museum of
Natural History, examined all the photographs for me in
order to see if she could ascertain the sex and age of
the skeletons. In many cases this was very difficult
because pertinent features were obscured from view, but
she was able to make some tentative observations on sex,
define the juveniles and adolescents among the burial
population, and confirm that there were adult males,
females and juveniles present. I decided to incorporate
her identifications in the following attempt to analyse
this group of graves, but it should be stressed again
that the ageing and sexing of the bodies is based solely
on an examination of the available photographs, and
therefore cannot be taken as more than an indication.
Even without the following analysis, it will be noted
that the richest grave in this group, no. 66, from the
number of objects alone, is that of a child, Gerzean in
date, situated beneath the gateway of the Fort. In
addition to the mass of pottery, it contained a slate
palette in the shape of a falcon (not found), some
copper objects (LM.25.11.05.49 & 50) and a bone comb
with archaic falcon decoration (LM.25.11.05.48) on the
child's head. A Naqada III grave (no. 107), which also
had a large quantity of pots, was a double burial.

The following analyses and observation were checked and
commented on by Professor Fekri Hassan, whose timely
contribution at this interpretive stage was extremely
helpful.

Observations

The conclusions that can be drawn from the following
analysis of the relatively few graves exposed in
Garstang's excavation are those which would be expected.
The majority of the graves were Naqada III/Dynasty I in
date, which is probably a result of the restriction of
the excavation within the Fort walls, as earlier graves
were discovered outside it to the east by the Lansing
expedition, although the greater number of graves dated
to Naqada III may indicate an increase in population.
All the burials were in the crouched position. The
majority of the graves were oval, with a slight increase
in the rectangular graves in Naqada III. Most of the
graves were less than 1.50 m. long with no major increase
in size by Naqada III/Dynasty I. The majority of bodies,
where the orientation could be determined, had the head
south and face west in both phases, which is of course

the normal position in most middle and late Predynastic
graves in Egypt. The overall percentage obtained from
Garstang's records for this orientation of the bodies is,
however, less than that at Naqada (64.8% to 96.4% of the
total), which may be an indication of sloppy recording
methods, but is more likely to be in accordance with the
trend observed at other sites of reversion to the head
north and face east orientation of the Early Predynastic
(Badarian) during the Early Dynastic period (Castillos,
1982, particularly Table 4), after a period of orthodoxy
(head south, face west) in the Naqada I/II periods.   As
the percentages for orientation are not available for
the graves of Naqada III/Dynasty I at Naqada and therefore could not be incorporated by Castillos in his
analysis of cemeteries, it is hoped that a study of the
newly 'discovered' Ballas (Quibell) notebooks in the
Petrie Museum (see Chapter I and Bourriau, 1984) will be
an aid in the completion of the recording and analysis
of cemeteries of that date in the area (Adams and Hassan,
forthcoming).

There were very few rich graves, as defined by the
number of objects. In both periods the majority had ten
objects or less, with about twenty-five percent of the
graves in the 'middle class' range. Size seems to have
had nothing to do with the number of objects in the
graves; the percentages are equal in the smaller and
larger graves. Exotic objects such as copper bracelets
and tools, beads, shells, bone combs and stone vases
occurred in small quantities in fifty-one (36%) of the
graves, with no significant increase in the later phase,
while flints were found in only thirteen graves.

There was very little B (black-topped red) ware pottery
in the cemetery. The R (rough) and D (decorated) wares,
dominant in Naqada II graves, are replaced by an increase
in W (wavy handled) ware and L (late and Protodynastic)
ware in Naqada III/Dynasty I; the usual chronological
indicators in the phases of the Predynastic and Protodynastic. Slate palettes occurred with equal frequency
in both phases showing the evolutionary change from
zoomorphic bird and fish shapes (the most frequent) to
the rectangular shapes of Dynasty I.

The comparisons of wealth, grave size and sex are
totally inconclusive due to the large number of adults
where the sex could not be determined. There does seem
to have been a preferential burial of adults (84.6% of
the total) since the ratio of adults should be in the
range of fifty to sixty percent of the population
(information courtesy of Fekri Hassan, see Pressat, R.,
Population, Penguin, 1971, p.24), which agrees with the
drop in the number of children observed by Castillos
(1982) in Late Predynastic and Early Dynastic cemeteries

elsewhere (to ten percent of the total). On the
available data, there was a sex ratio of 76.4 (number of
males per hundred females), indicating a preferential
interment of females. On these figures, it would seem
that there is no difference in size or wealth between
the graves of men and women and, as previously stated,
the grave with the greatest number and some of the most
exotic objects was that of a child.

GRAVE ANALYSIS TABLES

Number of occupants:

	One	Two	Three	None	Total of graves
Stufe II	33	O	1	1	35
Stufe III	92	6	O	2	100
Unknown date	7	O	O	O	7

Combined total of graves

142

Shape of graves:

	Round	Oval	Rectangular	Unknown	Total
Stufe II	1(2%)	29(82%)	4(11%)	1(2%)	35
Stufe III	O	87(86%)	12(11%)	1(2%)	100
Unknown date	O	6(86%)	O	1(2%)	7

Size of graves:

	A, less than 1.50 m long	B, more than 1.50 m long	Unknown	Total
Stufe II	24 (68%)	6 (17%)	5 (14%)	35
Stufe III	69 (68%)	25 (24%)	6 (06%)	100
Unknown date	5 (71%)	O	2 (86%)	7

Orientation of bodies:

Head Direction

	North	South	East	West	Unknown	Total of graves with bodies
Stufe II	8(23%)	19(54%)	2(05%)	1(02%)	4(11%)	34
Stufe III	12(12%)	65(66%)	11(11%)	3(03%)	7(07%)	98
Unknown date	1(14%)	6(85%)	O	O	O	7

Face Direction

	North	South	East	West	Unknown	Total of graves with bodies
Stufe II	5(14%)	O	7(20%)	16(45%)	6(17%)	34
Stufe III	5(05%)	12(12%)	10(10%)	46(46%)	25(25%)	98
Unknown date	1(15%)	O	O	6(85%)	O	7

Sex and Age:

	Children	Adolescents	Adult men	Adult women	Adults Uncertain
Stufe II & III	21(14%)	3(7%)	13(9%)	17(12%)	93(63%)

Total of bodies 147

Objects

I Occurrence of types in graves:

	B ware	R ware	P ware	D ware	W ware	L ware
Stufe II	4(12%)	28(80%)	10(28%)	13(37%)	10(28%)	8(22%)
Stufe III	2(01%)	66(65%)	15(14%)	4(03%)	51(50%)	86(84%)
Unknown date	O	2	O	O	O	O

	Palettes	Other
Stufe II	16(45%)	15(42%)
Stufe III	46(45%)	42(41%)
Unknown date	1	1

II Occurrence of other objects in graves;

	Flints	Beads	Shells	Copper objects	Combs
Stufe II	8(22%)	7(20%)	3(08%)	4(11%)	1(02%)
Stufe III	3(0.3%)	25(25%)	7(07%)	4(04%)	7(07%)
Unknown date	2	1	O	O	O

	Hairpins	Spoons	Bone pendants	Bone bracelets	Stone vases
Stufe II	2(05%)	1(2%)	0(0%)	0(0%)	3(08%)
Stufe III	7(07%)	0(0%)	1(01%)	3(03%)	7(07%)
Unknown date	O	O	O	O	O

	Mace heads	Total of graves
Stufe II	0(0%)	35
Stufe III	1(01%)	100
Unknown date	O	7

Wealth of the graves:

	0 to 10 objects	11 to 20 objects	More than 20 objects
Stufe II	25(71%)	9(26%)	1(03%)
Stufe III	69(68%)	28(27%)	4(03%)

Shape and size of graves:

Size A (less than 1.50 m long)

	Round	Oval	Rectangualar	Total of shaped and dated graves
Stufen II & III	1(.007%)	86(65%)	6(04%)	

Size B (more than 1.50 m long)

	Round	Oval	Rectangualar	Total of shaped and dated graves
Stufen II & III	0	22(16%)	9(06%)	133

Size and wealth of graves:

Size A

	0-10 objects	11-20 objects	More than 20 objects
Stufen II & III	76(61%)	18(14%)	2(01

Size B

	0-10 objects	11-20 objects	More than 20 objects	Total of sized and dated graves
Stufen II & III	8(06%)	17(13%)	3(02%)	124

Sex of the bodies and wealth of the graves:

Stufen II & III

	0-10 objects	11-20 objects	More than 20 objects
Children	9	3	1
Adolescents	3	0	0
Adult men	8	2	0
Adult women	10	4	0
Double burials	0	3	1
Adults uncertain	64	27	2

Size of grave and sex of bodies:

Stufen II & III

Size A

Children	Adolescents	Adult men	Adult women	Double burials	Adults uncertain
13	3	6	13	0	56

Size B

Children	Adolescents	Adult men	Adult women	Double burials	Adults uncertain
0	0	3	2	3	25

Shape of grave and sex of bodies:

Stufen II & III

	Children	Adolescents	Adult men	Adult women	Double burials	Adults uncertain
Round;	1	O	O	O	O	O
Oval:	15	2	8	14	1	O
Rectangular:	O	1	1	O	2	12

Dates of graves and orientation of bodies:

	Head North, Face East	Head North, Face West	Head South, Face West	Other
Stufe II	4 (11%)	2 (05%)	16 (45%)	7 (02%)
Stufe III	9 (08%)	3 (02%)	46 (45%)	10 (09%)

N.B. For the purposes of analysis, Stufe II/III graves were
grouped with Stufe III.

A Regional Perspective of the Predynastic Cemeteries of Hierakonpolis

by

Michael A. Hoffman
Earth Sciences and Resources Institute
University of South Carolina.

To complement Mrs. Adams' detailed presentation of the Garstang Fort Cemetery, I will consider the Predynastic cemeteries of Hierakonpolis from a *regional* point of view and focus on three theoretical aspects of the mortuary evidence: (1) population size, (2) cemetery patterning and (3) social stratification. All of these issues assume a broader significance for Egyptian history because of the central role played by Hierakonpolis in the evolution of the pharaonic state in the fourth millennium B.C.

Hierakonpolis is best described as a geographical region on the western bank of the Nile, embracing both the flood-plain and adjacent low desert. Most Predynastic and Early Dynastic sites cluster near the apex of a 10 km. long and 1.5 km. wide crescent-shaped alluvial embayment where it is intersected by a large wadi (Wadi Abul Suffian) that drains the late Pleistocene alluvial terraces and older Nubian sandstone inselbergs of the low desert. Strictly speaking, the ancient cultural area would have included El Kab on the opposite bank of the Nile and its surrounding territory - now being explored by a Belgian expedition.

Any estimation of the regional cemetery population depends on our ability to obtain a reasonable approximation of the number of Predynastic tombs in our area. Mrs. Adams' analysis provides a detailed picture of a small portion (ca. 5%) of the largest cemetery in the Hierakonpolis region. Most other Predynastic cemeteries in the area were looted in ancient times or around the turn of the century (Quibell and Green, 1902; Garstang, 1907) or so incompletely reported by early investigators (e.g. Quibell and Green, 1902; Adams, 1974b; H. de Morgan, 1909, 1912; Needler, 1984) that grave counts are impossible. To correct this deficiency, our own project has salvaged information from previously excavated and looted (occasionally the distinction blurs) cemeteries by mapping them and counting old grave depressions (Hoffman *et al*, 1982). In the case of the important elite cemetery at Locality 6, a detailed site map on the scale 1:250 was produced showing all tomb-like depressions and careful excavations undertaken (Hoffman *et al*, 1982, pp. 38-60).

I will now discuss my methods for achieving a tomb-based
regional population estimate for Predynastic Hierakonpolis
and then consider the problems raised by this approach.
From the outset it must be stressed that methods for
deducing numerical estimates are hampered by a sample
known to be incomplete. At least two large Predynastic
cemeteries existed which are now almost totally destroyed
- one near Mamariya at the downstream border of the
Hierakonpolis embayment (H. de Morgan, 1909, 1912;
Needler, 1984; Harlan, 1985) and one near El Sa'ayada at
the upstream border (Harlan, 1985). Vermeersch's excavations at El Kab (Vermeersch, 1978) and more recent
Belgian work there (Hendrickx, 1984) located one hundred
Protodynastic (Naqada III) tombs north-east of the
temple and within the Late Period walls. Finally, both
the old excavations of Quibell and Green (1902) and our
recent stratigraphic soundings below the town site of
Nekhen, now termed the Kom el Gemuwia by Fairservis,
(Hoffman, *forthcoming*; Fairservis,1986) suggest
extensive buried Predynastic settlements *and* cemeteries
exist under the modern flood-plain.

Table 1 lists surveyed Predynastic cemeteries in the core
of the Hierakonpolis region, estimates of their sizes in
square metres, dates, approximate number of graves and
evidence for internal social differentiation. Table 2
examines the ratio of square metres per grave in nine
human cemeteries where grave counts were possible.
Because such counts included a number of depressions of
questionable origin (i.e., looters' pits rather than
tombs), the ratios are presented in terms of high, mean
and low figures.

Unfortunately, due to extensive disturbance and drift
sand, grave counts could not be made at the two largest
cemeteries - Hk-27 (the "Fort Cemetery") and Hk-33 (the
"Painted Tomb Cemetery"). Since any regional cemetery
population estimate would be grossly incomplete without
figures for these sites, provisional estimates have been
derived based upon average high, mean and low density
ratios for all Hierakonpolis cemeteries from which data
were available. Tables 3 and 4 summarize my methods and
present estimates for the number of graves in localities
Hk-27 and Hk-33 respectively. The low density figure
employed was 81.2 m^2/grave (from Hk-30G), the high
density was 9.9 m^2/grave (from Hk-11), while an averaged
mean of 26.2 m^2/grave was used. The later figure was
also used as the low density ratio. As a rough control
on the ratios from Hierakonpolis, some figures from other
well known Predynastic cemeteries are presented in Table
5. Of these, only Nag-ed-Dêr 7000 with a high density
of 6.9 m^2/grave falls slightly above our high of 9.9.
As an additional control it was possible to employ Mrs.
Adams' study. For the total number of graves, we have

used *all* of Garstang's 188 burials, including Dynastic
tombs, since we are initially interested in a purely
areal formula and chronological corrections will be
applied later (Table 6).   To Garstang's 188 burials we
add two undisturbed Predynastic tombs discovered by
Fairservis in 1978 and 1981, giving a total of 190 for
the area of ca. 3600 m^2 encompassed within the Khasekhemwy Fort.   Dividing the total area by the number of
graves yields a ratio of 19 m^2/grave.   When this ratio
is then applied to the entire surface area of Hk-27
(see Table 1), an estimate of 3,602 graves is produced.
This figure is well within the range of 843 - 6,912 and
close to the mean of 2,612 obtained by our other tech-
nique based on regional averages (cf. Table 3).

Table 6 presents a comparison of grave frequency
estimates for all surveyed Predynastic cemeteries in
the core of the Hierakonpolis region.   Because Hk-27
includes a large Early Dynastic and an unknown
"Dynastic" component, the figures for the site have
been chronologically adjusted by halving all estimates.
The Pre- and Protodynastic tombs are assumed to account
for approximately half the life of the cemetery.

The overall number of Predynastic graves calculated for
all sites surveyed plus Hk-27 and Hk-33 ranges from
1,804 to 8,047, with an independent average of means
falling at 3,715.   These figures fall well within the
range calculated for the regional population based on
settlement data.   Unfortunately, the settlement-based
estimates postulated a large Early Predynastic population range of 2,544 to 10,922 for a point in time
(i.e., an archaeological generation), while the
cemetery-based figures embrace the entire Predynastic!

Considering that only a few thousand graves can be
postulated for a seven hundred year period at Hierakonpolis, any population estimate based on these would
be absurdly small.   Just how small is illustrated by a
recent study of our information by Professor Fekri
Hassan (personal communication).   Assuming a
tomb population of 3,000 and twenty years for an average age at death and the total years encompassed by the
local Predynastic sequence (ca. 700), Professor Hassan
produced a cemetery-based estimate of only 86 persons
per generation!   By using even the lowest figures (ca.
2,000 people) suggested by our settlement-based population estimates (Hoffman *et al*, 1982), Hassan is able
to show that even our most generous estimate of Predynastic graves (i.e., 8,047) is much too small.   For
example, assuming a local Predynastic population
starting at 1,000 and reaching 2,013 individuals seven
hundred years later and assuming an annual growth rate
of 1/1,000 and a death rate of 35/1,000, Hassan notes

that we should expect a total number of dead of 35,492.
Assuming a lower initial population of 500 people and
a growth rate of 2/1,000 (the death rate remains
constant at 35/1,000), we have a final population of
2,024 but a total number of dead of 26,736. When Hassan
assumed a beginning population of only 100 and a final
number of 3,282 people at the end of the Protodynastic
(Naqada III) with a growth rate of 5/1,000 and the same
death rate as before, he still had a total number of
dead of 22,390.

Professor Hassan (personal communication) explains the
huge discrepancy between the observed and expected
number of Predynastic graves as the result of preferential burial patterns which limited interment in the
cemeteries under consideration to members of the
privileged segments of society. Although agreeing that
some segments of the population, such as infants, are
selectively under-represented and that some adults may
not have been accorded what we think of as a "typical"
Predynastic burial, I feel that the range of wealth and
status differences in known Predynastic cemeteries
indicates interment of a representative cross-section
of the population. Furthermore, if there were a vast
under-class, then we would have expected to find at
least some of its humble tombs in the last ninety years
of Predynastic research (cf. the situation known for
the Old Kingdom).

While finding Professor Hassan's hypothesis intriguing
and worthy of more study, I prefer to emphasize diff-
erential preservation rather than social selection as
the main reason for the unusually low number of Predynastic graves. To illustrate the effects of preservation on the Predynastic archaeological record, we
have only to compare the two great centres of Hierakonpolis and Naqada. Although our estimated cemetery
population for Hierakonpolis compares favourably with
the 3,000 tombs known from Naqada and Ballas (Petrie &
Quibell, 1896; Baumgartel, 1970), the settlement remains
at Naqada and Ballas are miniscule when compared to
those from Hierakonpolis. Since the number and wealth
of its tombs indicates that the Naqada area possessed a
sizeable population comparable to that of Hierakonpolis,
erosion or alluviation must have destroyed or buried
many of its settlements.

In returning to the central issue of the relative valid-
ity of settlement-based versus cemetery-based Predynastic
population estimates (both, of course, are only gross
approximations), we must favour the higher range
suggested by the settlements for a number of reasons;
first, the paleodemographic estimates for such popula-
tions by Hassan (personal communication) indicate

gross under-representation of graves.   Second, modern
reliable excavated settlement data lend themselves to
much higher estimates (Hoffman *et al*, 1982).   Third,
ethnographic precedent suggests that societies similar
to the Predynastic in complexity had regional popula-
tions in the thousands, not in the hundreds.   Given the
political, social and economic pre-eminence of the
Hierakonpolis region in the Predynastic, and its ulti-
mate success in forming the core of a large pre-
pharaonic state, a relatively large and dense population is pre-requisite.   Simply put, there is no method
by which a few hundred souls could have built Hierakonpolis into a state and generated the millions of
tons of prehistoric debris now littered across the face
of the desert.

Turning from population estimates to the question of
regional cemetery patterning, I will outline briefly
some ideas we are currently exploring about the
structural principles that governed the location and
organization of Predynastic graveyards in the Hierakonpolis region.   Modern anthropologists speculate
that early sedentary peoples may have used cemeteries
to establish their supernatural claims over an area and
define its boundaries (cf. Saxe, 1970).   In the Hierakonpolis embayment, especially during Early Predynastic
times, there is a clear boundary-like patterning of
cemeteries, with sites at the downstream and upstream
borders of cultivation at Mamariya and El Sa'ayada
respectively.   The central core of settlement around
the Wadi Abul Suffian is likewise defined by cemeteries
on its upstream and downstream and desert peripheries
(see map in Hoffman *et al*, 1982; Harlan, 1985).   Even
though Predynastic sites in the flood-plain are buried,
it is known that Early Predynastic burials were present
in that area as well (Quibell and Green, 1902; Adams,
1974b).   Patterning not only occurs between cemeteries,
but within cemeteries (for patterning at other sites
see Castillos, 1983).   At the elite Locality 6 graveyard,
large Early Predynastic graves were aligned within a
special precinct, and in Protodynastic times there is
evidence that the whole site was turned into a deliber-
ately planned royal necropolis (Hoffman *et al*, 1982;
Hoffman, 1983).   Such patterning is believed linked to
the evolving doctrine of the royal mortuary cult
(Hoffman, 1983).

A related phenomenon is the tendency for Predynastic
cemeteries in the Hierakonpolis region to nucleate
through time.   This parallels nicely trends in the
settlement system which seem to be related to the urban
growth of Nekhen and political centralization (Hoffman,
Hamroush and Allen, *forthcoming*).   By late Predynastic
times there is even evidence for a large cemetery

(Hk-33) surrounded by smaller outliers (Hk-30G, Hk-43,
Hk-44 and Hk-45) - a pattern directly analogous to the
evolving settlement hierarchy. The trend towards
cemetery nucleation culminates in the use of one large
graveyard, Hk-27 or the "Fort Cemetery" for the whole
region. The planning and centralization of cemeteries
at Hierakonpolis provides a backdrop for the third
parameter of regional mortuary systems - the rise of
social stratification.

Just as a growing state requires a fairly large and
dense population, so too certain internal social
changes must occur which favour the centralization of
wealth and decision-making power, and the legitimization
of that power. One of the best ways of measuring
archaeologically such social transformations (in Egypt
at least) is through the increasing size, elaboration
and wealth of elite tombs.

Although we have recovered an impressive range of high
status artifacts from the looted tombs of Locality 6
(Hoffman *et al*, 1982, pp. 38-60; Hoffman, 1983), these
are only partial collections and cannot be used statis-
tically to compare and contrast elite tombs from different Predynastic periods. Our best source of information for such comparisons is tomb size and elaboration.

To date, Hierakonpolis is unique in possessing a long
sequence of elite tomb development extending from late
Early Predynastic through Protodynastic times (ca.
3600/3500 - 3100 B.C.). We may summarize the charact-
eristics of these elite tombs as follows: (1) they are
grouped in special areas within larger cemeteries or
even totally isolated from poorer tombs; (2) they are
considerably larger and more elaborate than the mass of
contemporary tombs; (3) elite tombs show a consistent
increase in size through time (Table 8).

The statistical and chronological evidence for increasing
tomb size and elaboration amongst elite structures
(Table 8) argues eloquently for the development of an
essentially autochthonous ruling group in the Hierakonpolis region reaching back at least to ca. 3500 B.C.
This continuity is also reflected in the settlement
remains at Nekhen, where an unbroken stratigraphic
sequence extending back to the Badarian underlies the
Early Dynastic - Old Kingdom town (Hoffman, *forthcoming*).

Whether or not a "chief" or "king" was actually interred
in the large Predynastic tombs at Hierakonpolis is less
important than the fact that elite tombs exist and
evolve continuously down to the beginning of the First
Dynasty. Many pyramids and other so-called royal tombs
of the first six dynasties may have been cenotaphs -

merely symbolic tombs for the ruler. What is significant is that the act of building a large tomb affords a
ruler an opportunity to concentrate wealth, mobilize
labour, reward followers, display his leadership
abilities, augment prestige and reinforce legitimacy
(Hoffman, 1979, pp.320-336; Metcalf and Huntington, 1979;
Arens, 1984).

Table 8 displays the dimensions and floor areas of
selected elite tombs at Hierakonpolis from Early Predynastic, Late Predynastic and Protodynastic times and,
for comparative purposes, includes examples from Naqada
and Abydos. At Hierakonpolis there is significant
increase in size through time, culminating in Tomb 1
with a floor area of 22,750 m^2. We believe this tomb
dates to the very end of the Protodynastic era and perhaps belonged to King Scorpion. By contrast, the so-
called tomb of Narmer at Abydos, B10, now identified as
one of Aha's (no more than two generations later than
Tomb 1 at Hierakonpolis), enclosed a floor area nearly
five times as great (Reisner, 1936; Kaiser and Dreyer,
1982). Only a generation earlier (i.e., before Tomb 1)
at the Hk-6 elite cemetery, Tomb 11 had half the floor
area and one quarter the volume of Tomb 1, although
some of its still undug companions may be larger.
Approximately 150-200 years earlier (ca. 3300 B.C.), in
the Painted Tomb, Green's number 100 (Hk-33), the floor
area was sixty per cent less than that of Tomb 1, but
comparable to that of contemporary T-5 at Naqada, a Late
Predynastic tomb in the elite cemetery (cf. Petrie and
Quibell, pl. LXXXIII, 1896; Kemp, 1973). Approximately
two centuries before the Painted Tomb 100 and Naqada
T-5, and four hundred years earlier than Tomb 1, Tombs
3 and 6 at Hierakonpolis (and their still unexcavated
companions) constituted the largest Early Predynastic
tombs yet discovered in Egypt (Hoffman *et al*, 1982, pp.
50-53). Their floor areas (individually) were half
that of the Painted Tomb's and one-fifth that of Tomb 1.
Based purely on the criterion of floor size (and
ignoring the above-ground chapels that covered the
Protodynastic royal tombs), it is possible to suggest
that political power and wealth were centralized slowly
at first and then, by the end of the Protodynastic and
the beginning of Dynasty I, took off dramatically. The
implications of such a "multiplier effect" for the rise
of Egyptian civilization has already been raised
(Hoffman, 1979, pp.303-305).

Thanks to Mrs. Adams' analysis of the Garstang material,
it is possible to say that for the Predynastic period
the increasing wealth and size of elite tombs was
matched by the tombs of the more common folk. It seems
as if the political and economic expansion of Hierakonpolis was enriching many segments of the regional

population.   In a very small way, perhaps the graves of
the Fort Cemetery (Hk-27) housed retainers, artisans
and other dependants of the royal court, and are thus
comparable functionally to the Early Dynastic tombs of
the lower grade retainers of the Memphite court at
Helwan (Saad, 1945-7 and 1969).

Publications of Garstang's 1905 Fort Cemetery excavations at Hierakonpolis restores some important information long believed lost.   Mrs. Adams' detailed description and analysis of the tombs and grave goods is a
valuable service, especially in the light of our on-
going research at Hierakonpolis.

In this essay I have considered the broader context of
the vast Predynastic cemeteries at Hierakonpolis which
were (in number if not preservation) at least equal to
those of Naqada and Ballas.   I have focused on three
theoretical issues to try to show how the cemetery data
might be interpreted on a regional scale: (1) population size, (2) cemetery patterning, and (3) social
stratification.   Perforce, this is a brief and preliminary review, and there is much I could not consider
here.   We anticipate publishing a thorough treatment of
the Predynastic cemeteries of Hierakonpolis and the
mortuary system of which they were a part in future
monographs of the Hierakonpolis Expedition.   The account
presented by Mrs. Adams is a valuable first step in
that direction.

TABLES

Abbreviations:

EP   Early Predynastic = Badarian/Naqada I (Amratian)

LP   Late Predynastic = Naqada II (Gerzean)

Prt   Protodynastic   = Naqada III (Dynasty "O")

TABLE 1   COMPARISON OF PREDYNASTIC CEMETERIES AT HIERAKONPOLIS

Locality[1]	Size(m^2)	Date	No. graves	Evidence for social differentiation
6	7000	E.P. Prt.	200+(-400)	Aligned Amratian chiefly graves. Protodynastic 'royal' tombs, plus other large graves and stone tomb
11	2960	E.P.	250-300	All *small* circular to oval graves
12	1640+	E.P.	56+	Early Amratian (white cross-lined ware).
		Prt.	1	Large tombs, covered by piles of rocks, one slab-lined Prt. tomb site heavily eroded by feeder wadis
13	4961+	E.P.	243+	Amratian tombs, possibly smaller than in 12, site eroded by feeder wadis
27	68,432	L.P.- Archaic	269+ (L.P.- Prt. only)	Earliest (i.e. L.P. and Prt.) portion under Fort, latest portion toward 3 'Archaic mastabas'. Graves under Fort excavated by Garstang (1907), Lansing (1935) and Fairservis (1980) varied from small to medium-sized but *not* elite, date to L.P.-Prt. and number about 269
30G	1056	Prt.	12+ 1 large 13	Very large tombs - small tightly defined group + one large separated tomb
43	5875	L.P.	c.75-100	Small circular tombs
44	2464	L.P.	100-200	
45	1200	E.P. Ptolemaic component	c.100??	
33	31,266	L.P.	?	Extremely large L.P. cemetery in 'Town', drift sand and looting obscures size
58	400	E.P.- L.P.?	10-20	None
68	c.2400	E.P., Prt.	c.30-40	Animal cemetery - dogs in E.P. components, cattle in Prt. component

1 See topographical site map in Hoffman *et al*, 1982, endpiece.

TABLE 2   GRAVE DENSITY RATIOS IN THE PREDYNASTIC CEMETERIES
          OF HIERAKONPOLIS

Site	Raw Density ($\frac{Area}{Graves}$)	Ratios: Low	Mean	High
6	$\frac{7,000}{200-400}$	35	23.3	17.5
11	$\frac{2,960}{250-300}$	11.80	10.80	9.9
12	$\frac{1,640^+}{56+}$	-	29.30	-
13	$\frac{4,961^+}{243}$	-	20.40	-
27	$\frac{68,432}{269+x}$	(See Table 3)		
30G	$\frac{1,056}{13}$	-	81.20	-
43	$\frac{5,875}{75-100}$	78.3	67.10	58.75
44	$\frac{2,464}{100-200}$	24.6	16.40	12.30
45	$\frac{1,200}{100}$	-	12	-
58	$\frac{400}{10-20}$	40	30	20
68*	$\frac{2,400}{30-40}$	80	70	60
			26.20^+	

+   excludes figures from Hk-30G and Hk-68
*   animal cemeteries excluded - deleted from all calculations

TABLE 3   GRAVE ESTIMATES FOR HK-27 CEMETERY

Area: 68,432 m^2

Low ratio: 81.2 m^2/gr

Mean ratio: 26.2 m^2/gr

High ratio: 9.9 m^2/gr

Estimates of grave frequency:

Low ratio: $\dfrac{68,432}{81.2}$ =   843 graves

Mean ratio: $\dfrac{68,432}{26.6}$ =   2,612 graves

High ratio: $\dfrac{68,432}{9.9}$ =   6,912 graves

TABLE 4   GRAVE ESTIMATES FOR HK-33 CEMETERY

Area: 31,266 m^2

Low ratio: 81.2 m^2/gr

Mean ratio: 26.2 m^2/gr

High ratio: 9.9 m^2/gr

Estimates of grave frequency:

Low ratio: $\dfrac{31,266}{81.2}$ =   385 graves

Mean ratio: $\dfrac{31,266}{26.2}$ =   1,193 graves

High ratio: $\dfrac{31,266}{9.9}$ =   3,168 graves

TABLE 5   AREA PER GRAVE DENSITY RATIOS AT OTHER PREDYNASTIC
           CEMETERIES

Armant 1400-1500

    Area: 12,825 m^2

    Graves: 175

    Ratio: $\dfrac{12,825}{175}$ =   73.3

Armant 1300

    Area: 525 m^2

    Graves: 23

    Ratio: $\dfrac{525}{23}$ =   22.9

Nag-ed-Dêr 7000

    Area: ca. 4,400 m^2

    Graves: 634

    Ratio: $\dfrac{4,400}{634}$ =   6.9

Naqada

    Area: ca. 122,982

    Graves: ca. 2,200

    Ratio: $\dfrac{122,982}{2,200}$ =   55.9

TABLE 6   ESTIMATES OF PREDYNASTIC CEMETERY POPULATION AT
           HIERAKONPOLIS

Site	Estimated number of graves		
	Low	Mean	High
6[1]	200	300	400
11	200	250	300
12	-	57	-
13	-	243+	-
27[2]	843[2]	2,612[2]	6,912[2]
30G	-	13	-
43	75	88	100
44	100	150	200
45	-	100	-
33	385	1,193	3,158
58	10	15	20
Total	1,813	5,021	11,090
Chron.)^2 Corr. T.)	1,391	3,715	7,634

(1) Includes undetermined number of animal burials

(2) Chronological correction factor applied. Because Hk-27
     (the Fort Cemetery) was used ca. 700 years (ca. 3400-
     2700 B.C.), the estimated totals for this site are
     halved to yield probably Predynastic figures:
     Low = 422,   Mean = 1,306,   High = 3,456.

TABLE 7   ESTIMATED CEMETERY-BASED POPULATION RANGE BY SITE
           AND PERIOD

| Site | Estimated Population Range by Period | | | | | Later Dyns (O.K?) |
	EP	EP/LP	LP	Prt	Dyn I-II	
6[1]	100-200	O	O	100-200	O	O
11	O	200-300	O	O	O	O
12	56	O	O	1	O	O
13	243	O	O	O	O	O
27[2]	O	O	(422$^{(5)}$—3,456)[6]		(422—3,456)[7]	
30G	O	O	O	13	O	O
43[3]	O	O	75-100	O	O	O
44[3]	O	O	100-200	O	O	O
45[3]	O	O	100	O	O	O
33[3]	O	?	385-3,158	?	O	O
58	O	10-20	O	O	O	O
Sub-Totals	399-499	210-320	660-3,558	114-214[4] 3,456-x	(422 — 3,456)	
Totals	399-499	210-320	(1,082$^{(5)}$ — 7,228)		(422 —3,456)	

        x = Late Predynastic graves

(1) See Table 6, note 1

(2) See Table 6, note 2

(3) Part of a related complex

(4) Graves arbitrarily divided, half to each period

(5) Includes combined population figures for Hk-27

(6) Figure is combined estimate for LP and Prt periods

(7) Figure is combined estimate for Dyns. I & II and later O.K.
     periods

TABLE 8   COMPARISON OF ELITE TOMB SIZES FROM HIERAKONPOLIS WITH
           SELECTED EXAMPLES FROM NAQADA AND ABYDOS

Site/Tomb	L.	W.	Depth	Floor Area (m^2)	Volume (m^3)	Date
Hierakonpolis:						
Tomb 3	2.50	1,80	1.85	4.50	8.325	EP
Tomb 6	2.90	1.60	1.50	4.64	6.960	EP
Painted Tomb 100	4.50	2.00	1.50	9.00	13.50	LP
Tomb 11	5.00	2.40	1.025-1.750	12.00 ca.1.53 ca.0.50	ca.14.03	Prt
Tomb 1*	6.50	3.50	2.50	22.75	56.875	Prt Dyn 0
Tomb 10	4.70	1.90	1.90	8.93	16.967	Prt Dyn 0

* belong to same tomb group

Naqada:						
T-5					9.475	LP
Abydos:						
"Narmer" B10					103.4	Dyn 0/I
Aha B19					110.0	Dyn I

APPENDICES

APPENDIX A

HIERAKONPOLIS MANUSCRIPTS IN LIVERPOOL UNIVERSITY

Archive File

Document 1   Plan of Fort with some graves plotted

Document 2   Pencil plan of Fort on cardboard

Documents 3 & 4   2 excavation field notebooks with sketches
                     of graves, numbered i) and ii)

Reports File

1) Edfu Report, January 1905

        Resumé: Description of outlying cemeteries and those
                 near Fort.
                 Beginning of Fort cemetery excavation -
                 pottery, slate palettes, stone hammer, flint
                 knives.
                 Excavation in north-east corner of town and
                 various portions of enclosure - sherd with
                 name of Narmer, flint knives, stone vessel
                 fragments.

2) Report, February 1905

        Resumé: Excavation of Fort cemetery, 175 undisturbed
                 graves.
                 Excavation of palace, temple and town ceased
                 when ground became too hard.
                 List of museums to which sets of pots to be
                 sent.

6) Report, January 1906

        Resumé: Harold Jones started excavating in temple site
                 in December 1905 - lapis lazuli head, ivory
                 figures, base of statuette of an Inyotef,
                 inscribed stelae (Dynasty XII), fragment with
                 name of Khasekhemwy, mace heads, pottery,
                 copper objects, scarabs, etc.

APPENDIX B

HIERAKONPOLIS NEGATIVES IN LIVERPOOL UNIVERSITY

Negative Number	Site Location
H.1	Fort Grave 6
H.2	Fort Grave 7
H.3	Fort Grave 8
H.4	Fort Grave 9
H.5	Fort Grave 10
H.6	Fort Grave 10
H.7	Town, flints and hammer (LU.E6591)
H.8	Fort Grave 11
H.9	Fort Grave 12
H.10	Fort Grave 14
H.11	Fort Grave 16
H.12	Fort Grave 17
H.13	Fort Grave 18
H.14	Fort Grave 18
H.15	Fort Graves 19-20
H.16	Fort Graves 19-20
H.17	Fort Graves 19-20
H.18	Fort Grave 21
H.19	Fort Grave 22
H.20	Fort Grave 23
H.21	Fort Grave 24
H.22	Fort Grave 94
H.23	Fort Grave 25
H.24	Fort Grave 26
H.25	Fort Grave 27
H.26	Fort Grave 28
H.27	Fort Grave 29
H.28	Fort Grave 29
H.29	Fort Grave 138
H.30 & H.30a	Fort Grave 32
H.31	Fort Grave 32

H.32	Duplicate of H.30
H.33	Fort Grave 35
H.34	Duplicate of H.33
H.35	Fort Grave 36
H.36	Fort Grave 37
H.37	Fort Grave 42
H.38	Fort Grave 43
H.39	Fort Grave 47
H.40	Fort Grave 48
H.41	Fort Grave 49
H.42	Fort Grave 50
H.43	Fort Grave 52
H.44	Fort Grave 53
H.45	Fort Grave 51
H.46	Fort Grave 60
H.47	Fort Grave 62
H.48	Duplicate of H.47
H.49	Fort Grave 61
H.50	Fort Grave 65, granite pillar bases
H.51	Fort Grave 68
H.52	Fort Grave 68
H.53	Fort Grave 69
H.54	Fort Grave 70
H.55	Fort Grave 71
H.56	Fort Grave 72
H.57	Fort Grave 73
H.58	Fort Grave 74
H.59	Fort Grave 76
H.60	Fort Grave 78
H.61	Fort Grave 81
H.62	Fort Grave 85
H.63	Duplicate of H.62
H.64	Fort Grave 88
H.65	Fort Graves 88-89, brick structure in centre
H.66	Fort Grave 90

H.67	Above Grave 90, flint knife
H.68	Fort Grave 91
H.69	Fort Grave 92
H.70	Fort Grave 93
H.71	Fort Grave 95
H.72	Fort Grave 96
H.73	Fort Grave 97
H.74	Fort Grave 101
H.75	Fort Grave 107
H.76	Fort Grave 107
H.77	Fort Grave 110
H.78	Fort Graves 110-111
H.79	Fort Grave 140
H.80	Duplicate of H.79
H.81	Fort Grave 140
H.82	Fort Grave 141
H.83	Fort Grave 142
H.84	Fort Grave 146
H.85	Fort Grave 171
H.86	Fort Grave 56, brick structure in centre
H.87	Fort Grave 57
H.88	Fort Grave 63
H.89	Fort Grave 34
H.90	Object
H.91	Polished axe head
H.92	Polished axe head
H.93	Fort, interior S.E. corner
H.94	Fort, interior near S. wall
H.95	Fort Grave 108
H.96	Fort Grave 66
H.97	Site further south, strainer spoon
H.98	Decorated pots, Fort Graves 35 (LU.E3037) and 68 (LU.E3036)
H.99	Along Great Wadi near Locality 6 of recent excavations
H.100	Fort, exterior from N.W.

H.101	Fort, interior centre to W.
H.102	Fort, exterior from W.
H.103	Fort, exterior from E.
H.104	Fort, interior centre to W.
H.105	Town/Temple as left by previous excavators
H.106	Fort, foundations of wall
H.107	Fort, gateway
H.108	Fort, graves near S. wall, W. of gate, Harold Jones
H.109	Town, site no. 302
H.110	Duplicate of H.109
H.111	Town, site no. 303b
H.112	Town, site no. 303 (LM.25.11.05.53), site no. 307, site no. 304a
H.113	Town, site no. 304
H.114	Town, site no. 306
H.115	Town, site no. 313
H.116	Town, Dyn. II-III house, brick on stone foundations
H.117	Temple, unidentified
H.118	Temple, lapis lazuli figure (Ash.E1057)
H.119	Temple, unidentified
H.120	Temple, unidentified
H.121	Temple, unidentified
H.122	Temple, building stone of Dyn. XVIII temple, Tuthmosis III + falcon of Nekhen
H.123	Town, unidentified
H.124	Town, unidentified
H.125	Town, unidentified
H.126	Town, surface view, large building
H.127	Town, unidentified
H.128	Town unidentified
H.129	Town, unidentified
H.130	Town, unidentified
H.131	Town, unidentified
H.132	Temple, view of site

H.133	Town, unidentified.
H.134	Temple, reverse of H.122
H.135	Town, unidentified
H.136	Along Great Wadi near Locality 6, of recent excavations
H.138	Unidentified, "Hierakonpolis: looking N.E."
H.139	Temple, lapis lazuli statuette (Ash.E1057), site no. 519
H.140	Temple, lapis lazuli statuette (Ash.E1057)
H.141	New Kingdom Tomb Hill, along Great Wadi
H.143	Ruins of Hierakonpolis

APPENDIX C

DISTRIBUTION LISTS OF OBJECTS IN MUSEUMS

Museums   Abbreviation

Australia: The Australian Museum, Sydney   AMS
                The Nicholson Museum, University
                            of Sydney   NMS
                Western Australia Museum, Perth   WAM
                Macquarie University, Sydney   MU

Birmingham: City Museums and Art Gallery   Bir

Blackburn: Town Hall   Bla

Bolton: Central Museum and Art Gallery   Bol

Burnley: Townley Hall Museum   Bur

Carmathen: Carmathen Museum   Car

Glasgow: Museum and Art Galleries   Gla

Lincoln: City and County Museum   Lin

Liverpool: National Museums and Galleries on
                            Merseyside   L.M.
                School of Archaeology and Oriental
                    Studies, University of Liverpool   L.U.

London: British Museum   B.M.
                Victoria and Albert Museum   V.& A.

New Zealand: Otago Museum   Ot

Sheffield: Museums Department   Sh

Swansea: Royal Institution of South Wales   RISW
                Wellcome Museum, University College   Sw

                                        NN = no number

AUSTRALIAN MUSEUM, SYDNEY

On loan to Department of Ancient History, Macquarie University,
North Ryde, 2113 Sydney.

| E15630 (MU 1480) | Pottery dish, type R24m | 102F |
| | H: 4.5   D: 14.1 cm | |

E15643   Pottery vessel   F
On loan to Nicholson Museum, Sydney

| E15644 (MU 1476) | Pottery vessel, type R76h | F32 ? |
| | H: 25.7   D: 5.6 cm | |

| E15651 (MU 1454) | Pottery jar, type R57c | 87F |
| | H: 10.4   D: 5.6 cm | |

E15664   Pottery bowl,type L16b   F8

| E15668 (MU 1457) | Pottery dish | F52a |
| | H: 6.8   D: 19.7 cm | |

| E15669 (MU 1474) | Pottery vessel, type R81 | F52 |
| | H: 22.7   D; 17.1 cm | |

E15670   Pottery cylinder jar,   139/6F
                       type Proto 46F6
On loan to Nicholson

E15671 (MU 1477)   Pottery vessel wavy handled   76F
                       type ? Proto 45m
                       H: 21.3   D: 10.4 cm

E15673   Pottery vessel, type L59d   154F

| E15675 (MU 1461) | Pottery vessel, type L30p | 143F |
| | H: 45.9   D. rim: 9.0 cm | |

E15678   Pottery vessel   F
On loan to Nicholson

| E15680 (MU 1478) | Pottery dish | 1F |
| | H: 4.0   D: 11.1 cm | |

| E15681 (MU 1473) | Pottery dish, type R24m | 103F |
| | H: 5.6   D; 15.2 cm | |

| E15683 (MU 1475) | Pottery vessel, type P24m | F47 |
| | H: 9.9   D; 25.0 cm | |

THE NICHOLSON MUSEUM, UNIVERSITY OF SYDNEY

On loan from the Australian Museum, Sydney

AML 7 (E15670)   Painted cylinder vase, type W62   139Fb
                      H: 27.5 cm

AML 8 (E15643)   Painted pottery cylinder vase,   F
                      type W62

AML 9 (E15678)   Rough bowl
                      H: 9.0   D: 16.3 cm

WESTERN AUSTRALIA MUSEUM, PERTH

Anthropology Department

A225   Pottery jar, type L36b   F141
                      H: 36.0   D. of rim: 10.5 cm

A226   Pottery jar wavy line   F107
                      decoration, type Proto 46j
                      H: 22.5   D. of rim: 10.5 cm

A227   Pottery jar, type Proto 73f   F107
                      H: 36.0   D. of rim: 11.5 cm

A228   Pottery jar wavy line   F97
                      decoration, type Proto 45M
                      H: 23.5   D. of rim: 9.5 cm

A229   Painted cylinder vase,   F97
                      type Proto 46k
                      H: 27.5   D. of rim: 10.5 cm

A230   Rough pot, type R66a   F72
                      H: 12.0   D: 5.5 cm

A231   Rough bowl, type L17m   F152
                      H: 7.5   D. of rim: 16.0 cm

A232   Rough bowl, type L17n   F163
                      H: 5.0   D. of rim: 9.0 cm   probably F168

A233   Polished red vase, type P93b   F
                      H: 13.5   D. of rim: 7.5 cm

BIRMINGHAM, CITY MUSEUM AND ART GALLERY

Transferred from the V. & A. Museum to the B.M.

129'56 (V.&A.582.1905)	Pottery vase	106
130'56 (V.&A.583.1905)	Pottery dish	
131'56 (V.&A.584.1905)	Pottery bowl	
132'56 (V.&A.585.1905)	Pottery jar	6(? 6)F
133'56 (V.&A.587.1905)	Pottery jar	
134'56 (V.&A.588.1905)	Pottery jar	
135'56 (V.&A.590.1905)	Pottery vase	
136'56 (V.&A.591.1905)	Pottery vase	
137'56 (V.&A.592.1905)	Pottery vase	
138'56 (V.&A.594.1905)	Pottery bowl	
139'56 (V.&A.595.1905)	Pottery bowl	F
140'56 (V.&A.597.1905)	Pottery bowl	F
141'56 (V.&A.598.1905)	Pottery vase	
142'56 (V.&A.599.1905)	Pottery vase	
143'56 (V.&A.589.1905)	Pottery dish	
144'56 (V.&A.600.1905)	Pottery vase	

BLACKBURN, TOWN HALL

No museum numbers available

Large pottery jar, type ?Proto 63e H: 45.0 D: 12.0 cm	147F
Pottery jar, type L36a H: 43.0 D: 12.0 cm	88F
Pottery cylinder vase, type ?W80 H: 24.0 D: 11.0 base D: 6.0 cm	F126

Globular pottery jar, type R65c		158F
H: 14.0 D: 5.5 cm		
Large pottery bowl, red slipped interior		15F
H: 12.0 D: 28.0		
Base D: 8.0 cm		
Rough pottery jar		F
H: 12.5 D: 9.0 cm		
Small pottery bowl, rolled rim, type ?L25b		F125
H: 5.0 D: 11.0 cm		
Mis-shapen pottery bowl		F
H: 7.5 D: 17.0		
Base D: 8.0 cm		

BOLTON MUSEUM AND ART GALLERY

44.05.3	Polished red vase, type P84h	36F
	H: 10.4 D: 7.8 cm	
44.05.5	Polished red vase, type P93a	54F
44.05.6	Pottery dish, type R24m	107F
	H: 6.0 D: 15.5 cm	
44.05.7	Pottery cylinder vase, type Proto 46F6	149F
	H: 27.0 D: 11.0 cm	
44.05.12 on loan to Lincoln	Pottery dish, type P40	48F
44.05.14	Pottery jar, type L36b	147F
	H: 36.5 D: 16.0 cm	
44.05.16	Pottery jar, type R84c	(F14)
	H: 31.0 D: 14.5 cm	
44.05.22	Pottery jar, type R47g	37F
	H: 26.0 D: 14.5 cm	
44.05.28	Pottery vase, type R66p	65F
	H: 10.5 D: 6.5 cm	

44.05.32   Rough pottery cup,   F
                      type R3a
                      H: 9.5   D: 10.5 cm

44.05.34   Wavy handled jar,   F28
                      type W43
                      H: 22.0   D: 12.3 cm

BURNLEY, TOWNLEY HALL MUSEUM

EG 187, 190,   Net-painted cylinders with   NN
191, 193, 194   wavy line decoration,
                      type cf. W62

EG 241   Wavy-handled pot, type W43b   F25
                      H: 25.5   D: 14.5 cm

EG 242   Large pottery jar,   F68
                      type R84c-d
                      H: 30.0   D: 15.15 cm

EG 248   Pottery vase, type L53a   F92
                      H: 19.0   D: 19.5 cm

EG 318   Net-painted cylinder jar   NN

EG 327   Large pottery jar   F

EG 339   Sherd, ?R76d pot   93F

EG 398   Rough pottery dish,   30F
                      cf. type R33D
                      H: 6.0   D: 17.0 cm

CARMARTHEN MUSEUM

75.769   Cylinder vase with net-   F18
                      painted pattern, type W62
                      H: 25.5   D. rim: 10.0 cm

75.770   Cylinder vase, type Proto 50G   F144
                      H: 21.5   D. rim: 9.0 cm

75.771   Polished red vase, type P81b   NR153F
                      H: 8.5   D. rim: 4.0 cm

75.772   Pottery dish, type L12c   F51
                      H: 6.5   D. rim: 13.5 cm

75.773   Straw-tempered bowl, type R26c   140F
                      H: 6.5   D. rim: 16.0 cm

75.774	Black polished jar (?once black-topped red), type B81h H: 16.5 D. rim: 9.0 cm	F13
75.775	Straw-tempered cup, cf. type Proto .32L(2) H: 10.0 D. rim: 9.0 cm	F
75.776	Polished red vase, type P93a H: 11.0 D. rim: 4.0 cm	F46
75.781	Pottery vase, type R65c H: 13.5 D. rim: 5.0 cm	F

GLASGOW, MUSEUMS AND ART GALLERIES
===

'23 - 33 s,t,u	Pottery vases	NN
'23 - 33 v	Pottery vase	82F
'23 - 33 w	Pottery vase	73F
'23 - 33 x	Wavy-handled pottery vase	163F

LINCOLN, CITY AND COUNTY MUSEUM
===

2140.25 (Bolton 44.05.12)	Polished red pottery bowl, type P40	F48

LIVERPOOL, NATIONAL MUSEUMS AND GALLERIES ON MERSEYSIDE
===
(EX MERSEYSIDE COUNTY MUSEUMS)

Some objects were lost in bombing during the war

25.11.05.2	Net-painted cylinder vase	138F

Exchanged with Otago Museum 1913

25.11.05.15	Red ware pottery bowl D: 8.5 ins	F missing
25.11.05.16	Red ware pottery bowl H: 3⅝ ins	F
25.11.05.17	Pottery vase H: 5¼ ins	F
25.11.05.18	Pottery vase H: 4¾ ins	F65 redîm, missing

25.11.05.19	Painted pottery vase H: 3⅝ ins	158F missing
25.11.05.20	Red ware pottery vase H; 6¼ ins	112F missing
25.11.05.21	Red ware pottery vase H: 5¼ ins	58F redîm, missing
25.11.05.22	Red ware pottery vase, base missing	55F missing
25.11.05.23	Pottery vase H: 3⅝ ins	30F missing
25.11.05.24	Red ware pottery bowl, black inside	168F missing
25.11.05.25	Red ware pottery vase H: 15 ins	F
25.11.05.26	Red pottery vase, tapered bottom H: 12 ins	19F missing
25.11.05.27	Red ware pottery saucer	F
25.11.05.28	Red ware pottery bowl, darkened inside D: 6 ins	37F missing
25.11.05.29	Red ware pottery bowl D: 3½ ins	6F missing
25.11.05.30	Red ware pottery saucer	97F missing
25.11.05.31	Red ware pot-stand	F
25.11.05.32	Red ware vase, type P40e H: 9¾ ins	78F missing
25.11.05.33	Red ware bottle-shaped vase H: 8½ ins	④
25.11.05.34	Red ware vase with spout H: 6½ ins	④
25.11.05.39	Fish-shaped slate palette	F23
25.11.05.40	Double bird-shaped palette	④ 50a
25.11.05.41	Rectangular slate palette H: 8.0 L: 14.5 cm	④ F129

25.11.05.45 a,b,c	3 shell bracelets D: 6.2 cm	④ F138
25.11.05.46	4 bone pins: a) bird topped L:14.1 cm b) broken bird L:13.8 cm c) broken L:11.0 cm	F35, F69, F115
25.11.05.47	Bone spoon	5OF
25.11.05.48	Bone comb, lacking teeth	66F
25.11.05.49	Copper ring	66F
25.11.05.50	Copper fish-hook	66F
25.11.05.51	String of beads and shells	12O
25.11.05.52	String of beads	2OF
13.12.05.1	Painted pot H: 11 ins	F149 missing
13.12.05.2	Painted pot H: 8¾ ins	138F missing
13.12.05.3	Red ware pottery vase H: 8¾ ins	
13.12.05.4	Red ware pottery vase H: 3¾ ins	55F missing
13.12.05.5 Exchanged with Otago Museum, 1913	Red ware pottery vase H: 4 ins	F4
13.12.05.6	Red ware pottery bowl D; 4¾ ins	F66 missing
13.12.05.7	Red ware pottery bowl D: 4 ins	8F missing
13.12.05.8	Red ware pottery bowl D: 7½ ins	141F missing
13.12.05.9	Red ware pottery vase H: 3½ ins	66F missing
13.12.05.10	Slate palette L: 23.0 W: 14.7 cm	19
13.12.05.11 Exchanged with Otago Museum, 1913	Slate palette L: 7 ins	F142

13.12.05.12	Rectangular slate palette with incised line border L: 16.8 W: 11.5 cm	146
13.12.05.13	Perforated oval slate palette L: 14.0 W: 8.6 cm	150
13.12.05.14	Sub-oval slate palette L: 14.0 W: 9.6 cm	91
13.12.05.38	Shell bracelets	5 from F102
13.12.05.45	Shell bracelets	F138
16.11.06.135	Pottery vase H: 17 ins	107F
16.11.06.136	Pottery vase H: $15\frac{3}{4}$ ins	95F missing
16.11.06.137	Pottery vase H: $7\frac{1}{2}$ ins	F
16.11.06.138	Pottery vase H: $8\frac{1}{2}$ ins	F126 missing
16.11.06.139	Pottery vase H: $9\frac{3}{4}$ ins	F25 missing
16.11.06.140	Painted pottery vase	147 missing
16.11.06.141	Pottery vase, rim imperfect H: $8\frac{1}{2}$ ins	61F missing
30.86.3	Rough pottery bowl D; 7.0 cm	F16 ex-Grisewood Collection
30.86.6	Pink ware bowl D: 18.0 cm	20F ex-Grisewood Collection
30.86.7	Red ware bowl D: 11.0 cm	F66 ex-Grisewood Collection
49.47.633	Double bird slate palette L: 32.2 W: 15.4 cm	Bought from Garstang
1973.1.697	Half calcite bowl	F140 ex-Wellcome Colln.; ex-MacGregor Colln.4005, VI

LIVERPOOL, SCHOOL OF ARCHAEOLOGY AND ORIENTAL STUDIES

E252	Udjat eye, faience	41F
E718	Stone spindle whorl	F33T
E719	Stone pebble L: 5.6 cm	F56k
E720	Stone pebble L: 4.3 cm	83F
E721	Stone pebble L: 3.4 cm	F35
E807	Copper bracelet D: 7.0 cm	98F
E2516x	Alabaster pot H: 4.7 D: 4.8 cm	F146c
E2901	Cowrie shell	41F
E2902	Murex shell L: 14.5 W: 5.6 cm	91F
E2906	Shell, Iridina Nilotica Fer? L: 6.2 W: 2.3 cm	69F
E2914	Perforated shell, Iridina Nilotica Fer. L: 7.7 W: 2.7 cm	36F
E3031	Decorated pot, type D36 & D40m H: 8.1 D: 6.5 cm	(? F70g)
E3032	Decorated two-handled pottery vase, type D10c, dec. D8g H: 1.0 D: 5.7 cm	F42f
E3036	Theriomorphic decorated pottery vase, flamingoes, type F59t L: 12.0 H: 5.5 cm	(F68)
E3037	Theriomorphic decorated vase, wavy lines, cf. type F59p L: 10.4 H: 5.5 cm	(F35f)
E3302	Shell, Aetheria Caillaudi Fer, "Nile oyster" L: 6.7 cm	F161g

E4031	Red ware pottery vase, cf. type P91 H: 11.8 D: 7.0 cm	102F
E4032	Brown ware pot, strainer inside	
E4033	Brown ware pot, strainer inside, type 50a H: 25.0 D: 17.0 cm	31a
E4039	Red streak burnished bowl H: 10.0 D: 23.7 cm	
E4051	Red ware pottery vase, type F32d H: 10.0 W: 8.7 cm	42g
E4052	Red polished pot, type P75d H: 3.9 D: 3.8 cm	F66c
E4053	Red polished pot, type P95d H: 10.0 D: 6.5 cm	F66v
E4083	Brown ware pottery vase, type P40c H: 24.5 D: 13.7 cm	42y
E4227	Pottery dish, type P24k D: 18.5 H: 6.4 cm	33
E4279	Small pottery saucer, type L7a D: 12.7 H: 3.4 cm	66
E4307	Egg-shaped pottery vase H: 18.0 D: 10.8 cm	66/z
E4310	Black topped red jar	Purchased at Hierakonpolis
E4330	Elongated pottery vase with painted wavy lines, type Proto. 63b H: 21.6 D: 11.0 cm	12
E4430	Globular pot, type L53r H: 7.2 D: 7.0 cm	F24b
E4431	Oval pot, type P93c H: 10.6 cm	50a
E4434	Globular pot, type P93a H: 11.3 D: 8.8 cm	136c
E4454	Oval pot, type P95b H: 10.7 D: 7.0 cm	42x

E4475	Globular vase H: 11.7 cm	
E4539	Globular pot with painted decoration, cf. type Proto 94k H: 19.0 D: 13.4 cm	101
E4593	Small hemispherical bowl, type P1c H: 6.5 D: 10.0 cm	168
E4663	Red ware bowl, type R23d D: 10.0 H: 4.0 cm	68
E4890	Tall narrow storage jar, type L36a H: 43.0 cm	151a
E5307	Fish-shaped slate palette L: 14.3 W: 74.0 cm	69F
E5308a	Rectangular slate palette L: 12.7 W: 9.2 cm	F140
E5308b	Brown pebble L: 5.0 cm	? 140F
E5317	Brown pebble	
E5338	Slate palette L: 21.2 H: 13.7 cm	F66r
E5339	Slate palette L: 12.7 W: 10.8 cm	F96m
E5341	Slate palette L: 17.2 H: 11.3 cm	F90e
E5344	Slate palette 20.3 x 10.2 cm	(?? 107F)
E5345	Slate palette, sub-rectangular L: 10.5 W: 8.2 cm	(?F)
E5346	Slate palette, oval D: 12.4 cm	(?? F125)
E5349	Slate palette L: 8.9 W: 7.0 cm	(?F)
E5350	Slate palette L: 15.2 W: 8.0 cm	(?F)

E5351	Fish-shaped slate palette, broken L: 17.2 W: 12.0 cm	(?? F10)
E5352	Fragment slate palette with incised line border L: '9.0 W: 5.7 cm	(?F)
E5353	Slate palette fragment with incised line border L: 10.9 W: 7.3 cm	(?F)
E5354	Slate palette fragment with incised line border L: 5.7 W: 6.0 cm	(?F)
E5355a-b	Two slate palette fragments with incised line border L: 6.5; 5.5 cm	(?F)
E5356	Slate palette fragment with incised line border L: 6.5 cm	(?F)
E5359	Slate palette L: 10.5 W: 5.2 cm	F136
E5362	Slate palette fragment L: 7.5 W: 5.6 cm	(?F)
E5366	Slate palette fragment L: 12.7 W: 8.0 cm	(?F)
E5367	Slate palette L: 6.3 W: 5.8 cm	(?F)
E5368	Slate palette fragment L: 7.0 W: 6.0 cm	(?F)
E5369	Slate palette fragment L: 11.3 W: 7.3 cm	(?F)
E5370	Slate palette L: 7.1 W: 4.0 cm	(?F)
E5372	Slate palette L: 12.5 W: 6.6 cm	F.H.
E5373	Slate palette L: 10.7 W: 9.5 cm	(?F)
E5374	Slate palette L: 13.6 W: 11.0 cm	F38b

E5379	Slate palette L: 16.1 W: 9.4 cm	F13
E5380	Slate palette L: 5.6 W: 4.8 cm	F49c
E5381	Slate palette L: 12.0 W: 6.7 cm	F36a
E5382	Slate palette L: 16.3 W: 8.6 cm	F62e
E6084	Red egg-shaped pottery jar, type P40e H: 25.0 D: 11.8 cm	87
E6086	Pottery vase, type P97k H: 21.4 D: 11.8 cm	168f
E6087	Red polished pottery bottle, type P56a H: 22.0 cm	
E6088	Net-painted pottery cylinder vase, type W62 H: 24.5 D: 10.5 cm	72
E6091	Pottery vase, type Proto 65u H: 23.0 D: 9.0 cm	145g
E6094	Small egg-shaped pottery vase, wavy line painted decoration, cf. type D10k H: 12.3 D: 8.9 cm	F50
E6095	Small globular pottery vase, undecorated, type D41b H: 9.8 D: 9.5 cm	44
E6099	Small oval pottery vase, decorated, type D10k H: 10.0 D: 7.3 cm	136c
E6100	Small globular pot, type P75i H: 4.2 D: 4.1 cm	66e
E6106	Pottery storage jar, type L30p H: 42.0 cm	132b
E6111	Painted lug-handled pot, decorated with birds H: 13.7 D: 22.0 cm	(?F)

E6116	Large pottery jar, type Proto 7Op H: 35.0 D: 14.0 cm	107
E6203	Black topped elongated vase, type B58a H: c.40.0 cm	92
E6433	Small decorated bowl with lugs, type D671 H: 7.0 cm	? F47h
E6591	Half stone hammer L: 66.0 cm	Garstang, 1907, pl.VII, 1.
E6610	Flint blade, worn L: 6.2 cm	66
E6617	Flint fish tail L: 6.5 cm	over 66
E6620	Flint flake L: 4.5 cm	F66
E6622	Flint flake L: 5.6 cm	F66
E6623	Flint blade L: 6.5 cm	F33
E6637	Flint flake L: 4.7 W: 5.5 cm	F65
E6638	Flint flake L: 10.2 W: 3.7 cm	F163
E6855	Decorated pottery vase H: 10.2 D: 17.2 cm	70
E6859	Wavy handled pottery vase, type W19 H: 24.0 D: 15.5 cm	66b
E6861	Pottery cylinder vase, type Proto 46F6 H: 24.0 D: 11.4 cm	149f
E6863	Pottery cylinder jar, type Proto 46F6 H: 23.5 D: 11.1 cm	141
E6865	Small squat pottery vase, type D1t H: 5.2 D: 7.2 cm	42f

E6867	Pottery vase decorated with red spots, type D63c H: 7.2 D: 8.5 cm	(? F35)
E6967	Red ware cylinder vase with two potmarks H: 18.0 cm	?F
E7261	Tapering bone, bull rib L: 17.3 W: 2.1 cm	7OF
E7262	Shell bracelet D: 2.1 cm	F102

LONDON, BRITISH MUSEUM

42079	Net painted cylinder jar, type Proto 46d8 H: 29.8 D: 11.8 cm	F126
42080	Net painted cylinder jar, type Proto 46d2 H: 30.0 D: 11.0 cm	F Ex-Hilton Price Colln.
42081	Wavy handled cylinder vase, type W47a H: 20.3 D: 9.8 cm	81F
42082	Streak burnished jar, cf. type P97k & Proto 65w H: 19.0 D: 11.8 cm	103F
42090	Rough jar, tapered base H: 41.6 D: 12.6 cm	F
42091	Rough drop pot H: 12.6 D: 10.3 cm	F
42092	Pink pottery jar with potmark H: 20.3 D: 8.6 cm	F Spencer, 1980, Cat. no. 311
42093	Rough pottery jar, type R57e H: 6.3 D: 7.4 cm	157F
42094	Red polished drop pot, cf. type P93a H: 10.6 D: 8.9 cm	79F
42095	Rough jar, pointed base H: 25.0 D: 13.5 cm	F Spencer, 1980, Cat. no. 304

42096	Rough mis-shaped pottery vase with potmark H: 7.5 D: 6.0 cm	probably 152F
42097	Rough pottery vase, type R65b H: 11.0 D: 8.9 cm	154F
42131	Red dish, polished interior, cf. type L16b H: 9.9 D: 25.7 cm	36F
42132	Rough flared pottery bowl, type Proto 5f H: 9.1 D: 15.0 cm	107F
42133	Pink ware pottery bowl, type Proto 17n H: 9.0 D: 17.3 cm	168F

LONDON, VICTORIA AND ALBERT MUSEUM

593-1905	Net painted pottery cylinder jar	157F
596-1905	Pot	

transferred to British Museum in 1956

NEW ZEALAND, OTAGO MUSEUM

Exchanged from Liverpool (Merseyside Museum), 1913

D13.46 (25.11.05.2)	Net painted cylinder vase	138F
(13.12.05.11)	Slate palette	F142
(13.12.05.5)	Pot	

SHEFFIELD, MUSEUMS DEPARTMENT

J1905.88	Buff rolled rim jar, type ?Proto 81f H: 52.5 D. of rim: 13.7 cm	143F
J1905.89	Wavy line cylinder jar, type ?W61 H: 50.0 D. of rim: 11.8 cm	167F

J1905.90	Globular buff pottery jar, type ? R55a H: 7.5 D: 3.7 cm	F30a
J1905.91	Red ware pottery dish, cf. type L7c H: 5.6 D: 16.2 cm	30F
J1905.93	Red ware pottery disc H: 7.5 D: 18.1 cm	107F
J1905.94	Wavy line buff pottery jar, type ? W51a H: 23.1 D: 11.2 cm	F129
J1905.95	Net painted pottery cylinder jar, type ? W62 H: 30.0 D: 10.6 cm	151F
J1905.96	Red ware pottery jar, type ? R84 H: 26.2 D. of rim: 12.5 cm	F129e
J1905.97	Wavy line pottery vase, type ?W51a H: 20.0 D. of rim: 9.3 cm	F133

SWANSEA, ROYAL INSTITUTION OF SOUTH WALES

AX121.1	Wavy handled pottery jar H: 24.8 D: 15.2 cm	F
AX121.3	Pottery storage jar, tapered base	F
AX121.4	Pottery storage jar, tapered base type L36n H: 38.5 D: 16.0 cm	149F
AX121.5	Flat base pottery jar, type Proto 70m H: 29.5 D: 15.5 cm	107F
AX121.6	Pottery bowl, type L16b D: 18.7 H: 9.7 cm	119F
AX121.7	Pottery cylinder jar, type W80 H: 23.3 D: 11.4 cm	F146
AX121.8	Painted pottery vase, neck missing, cf. type D20 H: 11.3 D: 12.5 cm	157F

AX121.10   Small pottery vase   F
                  H: 11.7   D: 8.4 cm

AX121.11   Pottery vase, type R66p   90F
                  H: 11.7   D: 8.6 cm

AX121.12   Broken pottery dish,   143F
                  type ? R26a

SWANSEA, WELLCOME MUSEUM, UNIVERSITY COLLEGE

W1046   Decorated lug handled pot,   ? 137F
                  type D7c
                  H: 9.2 cm

W1047   Streak burnished pottery plate,   60F
(Well. No.   type Proto 25d   (Ex-MacGregor
13459)   D: 26.2   H: 5.2 cm   Colln. 1705)

W1048   Wavy handled pot, type W42   F42
                  H: 11.8   W: 6.5 cm

APPENDIX D

ANCIENT HIERAKONPOLIS: ADDENDA AND CORRIGENDA

(For abbreviations see *Ancient Hierakonpolis*, pp. xix-xx)

p. xx:

Add 'Liv. National Museums and Galleries on Merseyside (ex Merseyside County Museums), Liverpool
    Maid. Maidstone Museum, Kent.'

Cat. No. 90:

There is an additional faience foundation plaque fragment like
UC.16248, with the names of Hatshepsut and Tuthmosis III, UC.8532.

Cat. Nos. 104, 148, 163, 214:

Provenance: East of Main Deposit in a pot in a circle of pots,
see *Hk* II, p. 36.

Cat. No. 126:

Parallel: Ash.E208 from Abydos Temple Deposit M69, Petrie, W.M.F.,
Abydos II, 1903, pl. IX, 189, see *AH*, pl. 23.   BM.38020 is also
from this deposit.

Cat. No. 149:

Delete Site number 147, insert Site numbers 146, 122 and 163.

Cat. No. 191:

Site no. 400, Ash.E1040 also has this Site number and it is from
the Temple, not the Main Deposit, see *Hk* II, p.38, therefore this
gold leaf is also from the Temple Area.

Cat. No. 283:

Parallel: Petrie *et al, Tarkhan* I, 1913, pl. LVIII, 99d, S.D.77,
C/Fitz.E27.1912.

Cat. Nos. 322 and 323:

The museum number for *Hk* II, pl. LXIII, 16, is Ash.E4010.

Cat. No. 350:

Under Comment: The inscribed stone bowl, *Hk* II, pl. XLVIIIa should
be C/Fitz.E23.1898, not Ash.E23.

p. 85, Index:

for 17515 read 16515
for 20556 read 17556
for 27533 read 20553
for 11469 read 27469   in lower right column.

ANCIENT HIERAKONPOLIS SUPPLEMENT: ADDENDA AND CORRIGENDA

MAR = Manuscript Analysis Register

p. 5:

After "the scale is not uniform except for the pottery types from
Petrie's *Naqada and Ballas* when the scale is" insert "1:9 and the
scale of the stone vase types is 1:6".

p.6:

MAR, Site no, 42, the inscribed stone bowl is C/Fitz.E23.1898, not
Ash.E23, see p. 128 (pl. XLVIIIa reproduction, col. II).

MAR, Site no. 216, Ash.E3647 should be added to this entry; it is
another cup with finger divisions like Ash.E4007.

The serpentine boat with snakes under it is Ash.E119, therefore
delete the entry from the Provenance Index, p. 165, under Main
Deposit, No Number.

p. 7:

MAR Site no. 433, the objects entry should read:

    Faience bird, UC.15031 (Cat. No. 104)
    Faience shrine, UC.11017 (Cat. No. 148)
    Faience pot, UC.15004 (Cat. No. 214)
    Faience pot on stand, UC.15011 (Cat. No. 163)

MAR, Site no. 434, no. 7 is Ash.E125, see p. 129 (pl. XLVIIIa
reproduction, col. III), therefore delete from the Provenance
Index, p. 165, under Main Deposit, No Number.

p. 9:

MAR, Site no. 453.65, the steatite bottle is Ash.E120, see p. 127
(pl. XLVIIIa reproduction, col. III), therefore delete from
Provenance Index, p. 165 under Main Deposit, No Number.

p. 11:

MAR, Site no. 471.5, the steatite duck vase is Ash.E2808, see p.
130 (pl. XLVIIIb reproduction, col. I). Ash.E2809 is a headless
alabaster duck vase marked 471.5. Delete Ash.E2808 from the
Provenance Index, p. 165, under Main Deposit, No Number.
C/Fitz.E9.1898 is a serpentine example, see *Hk* I, pl. XX, 2.

p. 12:

MAR, Site no.555.4, the basalt man is Ash.E9, the haematite figure
on p. 130 (pl. XLVIIIb reproduction, col. I), therefore delete
from the Provenance Index, p. 165, under Main Deposit, No Number.

p. 12 and p. 13:

MAR, Site no. 471.32 or 33, the double animal head mace, Ash.E134,
is also that mentioned on p. 13, NN, no. 3, so that this MSS entry

is also Site no. 471.32 or 33. Ash.E134 is on p. 127 (pl. XLVIIIa
reproduction, col. I), therefore delete from the Provenance Index,
p. 165, under Main Deposit, No Number.

p. 14:

MAR, Site no. 147, add Maidstone EA346 for "flint saw".

p. 23:

MAR, Site no. 15, the coarse pottery fish tail shape is probably
Ash.E4010, *Hk* II, pl. LXIII, 16, therefore delete from the
Provenance Index, p. 166, under Temple Area, No Number.

p. 24:

MAR, Site no. 18, add ?Maidstone EA340 for "long flint flake".

p. 25, p. 142:

Ash.1959.42 is not the knife illustrated in MAR, p. 25, Site no.
36, it is a plain blade, not a notched knife; it is listed
incorrectly here and on p. 142, Ashmolean list, as 1959.142.

p. 25, p. 132:

Ash.E198 is Site no. 453, not 43 as on p. 132 (pl. XLVIIIb
reproduction, col. III), therefore delete from MAR, p. 25, Site
no. 43.

p. 28:

MAR, Site no. 50, add a flint knife to the object column and this
reference: MSS 210, p. 6.

MAR, Site no. 71, the stela of Khasekhemwy is Cairo Ent. 33895;
the limestone statue fragment of Wazit (Djet) is Ash.E3634.

p. 30:

MAR, Site no. 82, add Maidstone EA316, a pebble.

p. 30:

MAR, Site no. 86, Ash.1959.149a is a flint blade, not a knife, so
it is not the one drawn in MSS 205, p. 91. np. 14; this is C/A-A
Z15578 as already queried in this entry.

p. 31:

MAR, Site no. 88, Ash.E3109, a red limestone statuette fragment, is
shown (as sandstone) in MSS 202, p. 189 (omitted from MAR), therefore delete from the Provenance Index, p. 168, under Unprovenanced
Objects. The omitted MAR entry, to be added to p. 31 is:

| 88 | Near small chambers about B100 | Lower part of sandstone statuette that from the costume appears to be early, the costume is | 202 p. 189 np. 47 (4/3/99) |

                                        only a belt with a knot
                                        in front. Ash.E3109

p. 31:

MAR, Site no. 98, add a flint sickle, Liv.56.20.85. The fragment
of porphyry vase of Khasekhemwy is Ash.E3119 and 1962.1.

p. 33:

MAR, Site no. 122, add a flint saw, Maidstone EA344.

pp. 33-34:

MAR, Site no. 125, the final notebook entry to complete this
section was omitted:

125	About .5 below black stratum	Flint ▷	205, p. 183 np. 47 (4/3/99)
	Black stratum	Copper ⌒	
		Fragt. dark clay with red marks	
		Flint ▭ ▭	
	Between wall of enclosure and wall of stuma	Bangle	
		Shell Bits clay seals inscribed	
	1.8 below surface in seal bearing stratum	Bit of copper	

p. 35:

MAR, Site no. 133, add Maidstone EA330 for "saw flint".

p. 36:

MAR, Site no. 137, Temple is an error. The number 60.137 on MSS
7 (Map) refers to the page reference for Site no, 60 in MSS 205,
see MAR, p. 20, it should therefore be deleted from Appendix 1a)
and 1b) and the map on the endpieces in *AH* and here.

p. 37:

MAR, Site no. 150, the MSS reference is omitted, it is: 205, p.
188, np. 24; 210, p. 6. The first knife in the objects column is
Phil.E4762. Ash.E1727, a limestone spindle whorl, is marked 150,
so it should be added to this entry, and the site number to the
Ashmolean list, p. 139, but deleted from the Provenance Index,
p. 166, under Town, No Number.

p. 38:

MAR, Site no. 164, add a circular flint scraper, Liv. 56.20.89.

P. 39:

MAR, Site no. 186, the flints, Ash.E1762 and E1763 are square-
ended so they should be moved to the bottom of the page (on floor
of room at 1) from above; the long flint flake is therefore
C/A-A.Z15616, as suggested.

p. 40, p. 161:

Phil.E4748 is Site no. 198, therefore add to MAR, p. 40 and the
Site number to Philadelphia list, p. 161.

p. 40:

MAR, Site no. 198, add another pottery spindle whorl, Maidstone
EA320.

P. 44:

MAR, Site no. 215, add flint knife, Maidstone EA339, and for
"numerous circular scrapers" add Maidstone EA341.

p. 49:

MAR, Site no. 1100, delete "west" insert "east".

MAR, Temple NN, the red granite offering table of Sesostris I is
Cairo 23010.

p. 56, p. 117:

Site no. 30 is a grave in the cemetery as well as a point outside
the Temple Enclosure, see MAR, p. 56, Appendix 1a), p. 117. This
is proved by a letter from Quibell in the Ashmolean archives
which gives it 5 cylinder jars as 46 b-d (*Proto-Corpus*), cylinder
beads of blue glaze (Ash.EE6), a chisel (Manch.2775) and an adze
of copper (Manch.2776), see p. 132 (pl. XLVIIIb reproduction,
col. III). The beads have been put erroneously in the Main
Deposit No Number section of the Provenance Index, p. 165; they
should be deleted from these entries.

p. 56:

MAR, Site no. 64, the boat with animal head, possibly from a grave,
is probably Ash.E2811, therefore delete from the Provenance Index,
p. 168, under Unprovenanced Objects.

p. 58:

Ash.1959.145a is Site no. 82 only, see Ashmolean List, p. 142, so
it should be deleted from MAR, Site no. 123, but left in MAR, p.
30, Site no. 82.

p. 59:

MAR, Site no. 124, add Liv.56.20.83, a flint sickle blade for
"much worked flint saw".

p. 59 or p. 60:

MAR, Site no. 160, add Liv.56.20.91 "flint blade" and Liv.56.20.194
"flint sickle", but see also Site no. 161, p. 60.

p. 64:

MAR, Site no. 209, add Maidstone EA330 for the flint.

p. 65:

MAR, Site no. 89, add Liv.56.20.66, flint blade scraper for "flint
flakes good quality", and ?Liv.56.20.82 as "flint with pot".

p. 68, p. 139:

Ash.E651 on MAR, p. 68, Site no. 144 and Ashmolean List, p. 139,
should be E3651.

p. 74:

MAR, Site no. 180 under "section" add Maidstone EA349 for bottom
left rectangular flint blade, and Maidstone EA348, unillustrated,
another rectangular flint saw.

p. 76:

MAR, Site no. 211, add ?Maidstone EA332 for fragment of flint knife.

p. 77:

MAR, Site no. 225, is also a Cemetery grave as well as the Town,
see Hk II, p. 26. C/Fitz.E68.1898 is probably from this grave
and not the Town. Grave 225 should therefore be added to
Appendix 1a) and 1b), p. 119, p. 124.

p. 82:

MAR, Site no. 126, add ?Liv.56.20.191 as second flint from left.

p. 84:

MAR, Grave 14, the slate bracelet is Ash.E200, not Ash.EE2, which
is the beads and crystal pendants. Ash.E200 should therefore be
added to the Ashmolean List, p. 136, with the same reference as
EE2, a letter from Quibell to Murray.

p. 86:

MAR, Site no. 100, the pot no.(12) is Ash.1959.452, not 1959.542
as listed at one point.

p. 87:

MAR, Site no. lO2, add Maidstone EAl for the fish slate palette, and Maidstone EA317, a pebble.

p. 89:

MAR, Grave 112, the pot on the stand in MSS 211 was merely a copy of *Naqada and Ballas*, pl. XXXIII, Grave 112, so the drawing does not apply to Grave 112 at Hierakonpolis.

p. 93:

MAR, Site no. 167, add Liv.56.20.87, a flint backed core as "4) on top flint flake". Add Maidstone EA14 for the P56a with the potmark.

p. 97:

MAR, Site no. 5O5, the pot with the potmark is Ash.E2942 from Grave 6O5, see MAR, p. llO, (add MSS 71 to the reference column), so delete the following from this entry: "with potmark Ash.E2942" and the potmark sketch. The Site no. for E2942 on the Ashmolean List, p. 14O, should also be changed to 6O5.

p. 98:

MAR, Site no. 522, add ?Maidstone EA13 for R68.

p. 99:

MAR, Site no. 525, add Maidstone EA3 for the pot B53a.

p. 1OO:

MAR, Site no. 536, add Maidstone EA5 for the pot R81b.

p. 1O2:

MAR, Site no. 547, add UC.36312 for the pot D5O.

p. 1O3:

MAR, Site no. 558, add ?Maidstone EA12 for the dish P16.

p. 1O7:

MAR, Site no. 582, add Maidstone EA2 for the pot B62a.

pp. 113-4, pp. 127-132:

The following pages are unnumbered:

pp. 113-4   Sketches of Objects in the Green Manuscripts without
            Site numbers.
pp. 127-132   Reproductions of pls. XLVIIIa and b from *Hk* II.

p. 114:

The labels for the pot drawings "Coarse red ?Cemetery" and "fine pink UC.27609" should be exchanged.

<u>p. 117</u>:

Appendix 1a) add ?Liv. under Identification Source for Site no. 14
Temple.

<u>p. 117, p. 124</u>:

Site no. 65 is omitted from Appendix 1a), p. 117 and 1b), p. 124,
it is Outlier, see *Hk* II, pl. LXIX, 12, p. 51.

<u>p. 117</u>:

Site no. 88. Outlier, should be ?East Trench, not North Trench.

<u>p. 118, p. 123</u>:

The following Site number identifications are additional and should
be added to Appendix 1a), p. 118 and 1b), p. 123:

    179   Town
    116   Town, delete from Appendix 1b), p. 124
    108   Town

The MAR entries were omitted, they are as follows:

179 Town House (should be p. 73)	Floor level in hole in floor, near rough tray of last work	scraper Bit copper chisel	205, p. 223. np. 47
116 Town House (should be p. 67)	Outside wall of Room 4, .6 below surface	Fragts. alab. wavy handled vases, ?inscribed	205, p.240
108 Town House (should be p. 67)	Higher level than that of floor of room	OK pottery and stone as well as flints, lime- stone spindle whorl with C/A-A.Z15732	205, p. 230, np. 47

Site no. 116 is given as unidentified in Appendix 1a) and 1b).
Cairo 14680, a limestone grinder, has this Site number (add Site
number to Cairo list, p. 146), so it is from the town, therefore
it should be deleted from   the Unidentified List in the
Provenance Index, p. 167.

Site no. 108 is also a grave, see MAR, p. 89, but the incised
spindle whorl in the objects column, C/A-A.Z15732 comes from the
town, so delete it from the grave entry.

p. 118, p. 124:

Site no. 190 is Town, see MAR, p. 73, under Site no. 180.
C/Fac.LE170, a clay sealing, should be added to the objects
column, MAR, p. 75. The entries in Appendix 1a), p. 118 and 1b),
p. 124, should be amended and the Site no. deleted from the
Provenance Index, p. 167, under Unidentified Site Numbers.

p. 119, p. 167:

Add 255 Unidentified UC on p. 119 and 255 UC.19433 (an unpublished
Roman pot) on p. 167.

p. 119, p. 123:

Ash.E1040 is Site no. 400 from the Temple, not the Main Deposit,
see *Hk* II, p. 38, therefore the entries in Appendix 1a), p. 119
and 1b), p. 123, should be corrected and the entry deleted from
the Provenance Index, p. 163, under Main Deposit.

p. 119, p. 124:

Site no. 222 is Town, not Cemetery, as in MAR, p. 96, see *Hk* II,
pl. LXXIII, therefore delete from Appendix 1a), p. 119, and 1b),
p. 124, and add to Appendix 1b), p. 123. Ash.1959.145i is Site no.
222, not 22 as in the Ashmolean List, p.142, so delete from MAR, p.
85.

p. 123:
Site no. 507B, Temple, should be 507 ∝ β

p. 127:

Delete "Reproduction Courtesy of Egypt Exploration Society".
Hierakonpolis I and II were Egyptian Research Account publications,
precursors to the British School of Archaeology in Egypt series,
the copyright of which rests with the Department of Egyptology,
University College London.

p. 127, p. 163:

Bost.98.1018 is Site no. 471, but it is probably not one of the
maceheads on p. 127 (pl. XLVIIIa reproduction, col. I), therefore
delete it from there and add to the Provenance Index, Main
Deposit 471, p. 163 (and Bost. to Appendix 1a), p. 119).

p. 127, pp. 164-5:

Bost.98.1020, see p. 127 (pl. XLVIIIa reproduction, col. I), is
Site no. 543, therefore delete from the Provenance Index under
Main Deposit, No Number, p. 165, and add to Main Deposit 543,
p. 164 (and Bost. to Appendix 1a), p. 119).

p. 127, p. 165:

Bost.98.1015 is Site no. 453.46, therefore delete from the
Provenance Index under Main Deposit, No Number, and add as Main
Deposit 453.46 on p. 163 (and add to Appendix 1a), p. 119).

p. 128, p. 164:

Bost.98.1011 is Site no. 543.15, see p. 128 (pl. XLVIIIa reproduction, col. II), therefore delete from the Provenance Index,
under Main Deposit, No Number, p. 165, and add as Main Deposit
543.15 on p. 164 (and to Appendix 1a), p. 120).

p. 128, p. 165:

Bost.98.1012 is Site no. 471, see p. 128 (pl. XLVIIIa reproduction,
col. II), therefore delete from the Provenance Index under Main
Deposit, No Number, and add to Main Deposit, 471, p. 163.

p. 129, p. 165:

Phil.E3834 is Site no. 471, see p. 129 (pl. XLVIIIa reproduction,
col. II), therefore delete from the Provenance Index, p. 165,
under Main Deposit, No Number, and add to Main Deposit 471, p. 163
(and add to Appendix 1a), p. 119).

p. 130:

Add 22 faience beads, Bost.98.1010 to p. 130 (pl. XLVIIIb reproduction, col. I, base), and 13 faience beads, Cairo JdE 46498.

p. 130, p. 163:

Phil.E3915 is marked 68 and ?(4)7(1).5, see p. 130 (pl. XLVIIIb
reproduction, col. I). All the objects listed on p. 167,
Provenance Index under Unidentified Site Numbers with this
number are likely to be from the Main Deposit, therefore add on
p. 163 under Main Deposit (and alter in Appendix 1a), p. 117).

p. 130, p. 165:

Bost.98.1013 is Site no. 471.37, therefore delete from the
Provenance Index under Main Deposit, No Number, and add as Main
Deposit 471.37 on p. 164 (and to Appendix 1a), p. 120).

p. 131, p. 165:

Ash.E196 is Site no. 471.5, see p. 131 (pl. XLVIIIb reproduction,
col. II), therefore delete from the Provenance Index, p. 165,
under Main Deposit, No Number, and add to Main Deposit 471, p. 163.

p. 132, p. 165:

Bost.98.1009 is Site no. 10.471, see p. 132 (pl. XLVIIIb reproduction, col. III), therefore delete from the Provenance Index
under Main Deposit 10.471 on p. 164 (and Bost. to Appendix 1a)).
This baboon is probably MAR, p. 11.

p. 133:

Appendix 3b) Distribution Lists, add "Merseyside County Museums,
Liverpool, and Maidstone Museum, Kent" below the Royal Scottish
Museum, Edinburgh.

p. 134:

Delete Ash.E108 from the list on p. 134, it appears on p. 130
(pl. XLVIIIb reproduction, col. I).

p. 135, p. 163:

Ash.E127 is not Main Deposit Site no. 4, it is doubtfully marked
(?1)4 and it is New Kingdom, therefore delete from Provenance
Index under Main Deposit and amend the Ashmolean List, p. 135.

p. 135, p. 166:

Ash.E117 is from the Main Deposit, not the Citadel, therefore
delete from p. 166, Provenance Index under Citadel and add to
p. 165 under Main Deposit, No Number. It should also be added to
the Ashmolean List, p. 135, as:

E117   Fragment of alabaster vase,   *Hk* I, pl. XXXVII, 3
       inscription of Khasekhemwy.   *Hk* II, p. 31, p. 44
       H: 158mm   W: 167mm

p. 136:

Ashmolean List, the reference for E293 should be *Hk* I, pl. XXXIII,
p. 11; *Hk* II, p. 43.

p. 141:

Ashmolean List, delete E3631 which appears on p. 128 (pl. XLVIIIa
reproduction, col. II).

p. 145:

Cairo 14675 the plate reference is LXIII.2 not LXII.2.

p. 145:

Add Bost.98.1026, a headless greywacke statuette of a priest in
a leopard skin with cartouche of Seti I, and Bost.98.1027, an
inscribed statue fragment of a priest in a leopard skin, *Hk* I,
pl. XLVI.2. These are probably the second two statuettes of
priests published in the *Exhibition Catalogue*, p. 13, the other
two being in University College and Edinburgh.

p. 145, p. 167:

Add Bost.98.1023, a pebble, Site no. 25 to p. 145 and to the
Provenance Index under Unidentified Site Numbers, p. 167 (add
Bost. to Appendix 1a), p. 117).

p. 146, p. 163:

Cairo 14699 is Site no. 471, add to Main Deposit 471, p. 163.

pp. 147-155:

The following entries in the list of objects in the Museum of
Archaeology and Anthropology, Cambridge, are in the wrong order:

    p. 148   Z15203C   should be p. 147
    p. 152   Z15207A   should be p. 148
    p. 152   Z15208C   should be p. 148
    p. 151   Z15216E   should be p. 148

p. 149:

Cambridge Archaeology and Anthropology Museum List, the reference
for Z15621 is *Hk* II, p. 14.

p. 159:

Fitzwilliam List, E5.1900, the reference is *Hk* II, pl. LX, 2, and
E185.1900 is *Hk* II, p. 53.

p. 160:

Add the heading "National Museums and Galleries on Merseyside (ex-
Merseyside County Museums), Liverpool" above the University Museum
Manchester and the following entry:

    56.20.66   Flint blade scraper   89

    56.20.82   Flint sickle blade   89

    56.20.83   Flint sickle blade   124

    56.20.84   Flint sickle blade

    56.20.85   Flint sickle blade   98

    56.20.86   Denticulate flint flake   ?14 or ?74

    56.20.87   Backed flint core   167

    56.20.88   Backed flint scraper

    56.20.89   Circular flint scraper   164

    56.20.90   Circular flint scraper

    56.20.91   Rough flint blade   160

    56.20.93-   Microlithic flint   (see 110, 122, 146, 163)
       105   points and cores

    56.20.191   Flint sickle blade   ?129

    56.20.194   Flint sickle blade   160

    56.21.426   Forty-nine flint drills   (see 110, 122, 146, 163)
                for bead boring

p. 160:

Add the heading"Maidstone Museum, Kent" beneath the entry for
Liverpool and the following entry:

    "Objects donated to Maidstone by F. W. Green sometime after

the excavations at Hierakonpolis:

EA1	Slate palette L: 25.1 W: 15.6 cm	102	
EA2	Black topped pot type B62a H: 18.8 D: 17.0 cm	582	
EA3	Black topped pot type B53a H: 30.5 D: 17.6 cm	525/5	
EA5	Rough pot, type R81b H: 19.8 D: 11.8 cm	536	
EA12	Pottery bowl, type P16 H: 11.2 D: 26.6 cm	?558	
EA13	Rough pot, type R68 H: 11.8 D: 7.5 cm	?522 or 824	
EA14	Pot with potmark, type P56a H: 24.5 D: 14.7 cm	167	*Hk* II, pl. LXVII
EA316	Pebble L: 3.5 W: 2.6 cm	82	
EA317	Pebble L: 4.3 W: 4.2 cm	102	
EA318	Limestone spindle whorl H: 3.0 D: 4.3 cm		
EA319	Limestone spindle whorl H: 1.9 D: 3.6 cm		
EA320	Pottery spindle whorl H: 0.9 D: 3.6 cm	198	
EA321	Pottery spindle whorl H: 0.7 D: 2.8 cm		
EA324	Slate bracelet fragment L: 4.8 W: 0.6 cm		
EA325	Shell bracelet fragment L: 4.7 W: 0.8 cm		
EA326	Shell bracelet fragment L: 5.2 W: 1.4 cm		

EA 327   Shell bracelet fragment
          L: 4.4   W: 0.6 cm

EA329   Flint sickle fragment   99 or 49
          L: 3.9   W: 2.1 cm

EA330   Flint knife handle   209
          fragment
          L: 10.7   W: 3.4 cm

EA331   Flint knife fragment
          L: 6.5   W: 4.3 cm

EA332   Flint knife handle   ? 211
          fragment
          L: 6.7   W: 4.7 cm

EA333   Flint sickle fragment
          L: 8.2   W: 4.6 cm

EA334   Flint saw fragment
          L: 5.2   W: 2.8 cm

EA335   Flint saw fragment
          L: 6.0   W: 2.9 cm

EA336   Flint knife
          L: 3.7   W: 3.8 cm

EA337   Flint knife   "prehistoric"
          L: 10.0   W: 3.6 cm

EA338   Flint knife
          L: 8.8   W: 3.8 cm

EA339   Flint knife   215
          L: 11.6   W: 2.6 cm

EA340   Flint blade   (?) 8
          L: 12.5   W: 2.6 cm

EA341   Circular flint scraper   215
          L: 6.2   W: 5.1 cm

EA342   Flint core fragment
          L: 4.0   W: 4.3 cm

EA343   Flint core fragment
          L: 3.3   W: 1.9 cm

EA344   Flint saw   122
          L: 5.4   W: 1.6 cm

EA345	Flint saw L: 2.9 W: 1.4 cm	(?) 7
EA346	Flint saw L: 3.6 W: 1.1 cm	147
EA348	Rectangular flint blade L: 2.9 W: 1.4 cm	180
EA349	Rectangular flint blade L: 6.8 W: 2.4 cm	180
EA 350	Rectangular sickle blade L: 5.8 W: 2.2 cm	133

p. 161:

Philadelphia List, the reference for E4762 is *Hk* II, pl. LX, 2, and E4763 is *Hk* II, pl. LX, 3.

p. 161:

Phil.E3959 is also published in *Univ. Mus. Bull.*, XV (2-3), 1950, p. 30, fig. 14.

p. 162:

Phil.E4900, the reference is *Hk* I, pl. XII, 6, not pl. XXI.
Phil.E6620, the measurements are H: 0.15mm   W: 0.105mm.

p. 165:

Ash.E288 is Site no. 471.5 (add number to Ashmolean List, p. 136), therefore delete from Provenance Index, p. 165 under ?Main Deposit, and add to p. 164 under Main Deposit 471.5.

p. 166:

The following site numbers do not appear in the MAR, therefore these additions should be made to the Provenance Index, p. 166:

Above TEMPLE AREA - NO NUMBER:
"TEMPLE AREA
  400   UC.11032(191);   Ash.E1040" (and change to Temple Area in Appendix 1a), p. 119).

In CEMETERY GRAVES:
"30   Ash.EE6; Manch.2775, 2776

  225   C/Fitz.E68/1898"

Add numbers to Appendix 1a) and 1b).

P. 169:

Add Liv.   56.20.84
              56.20.88
              56.20.90
              56.20.92

Endpapers:

The following numbers should be deleted from the Temple plan on
the endpapers (see J. Crowfoot Payne, Review in *JEA* 61 (1975),
pp. 259-260):

    467, 525, 537, 505, 465, 491, 541, 507A, 507B, 517, 481,
    419, 502, 455, 433, 459, 418, 259, 465, 272

    517A, 517B, 243, 541, 137, 505, 459, 525, 505, 418, 433,
    481, 537, 507B, 507A, 455, 485, 502, 491, 465, 497, 259

    From left to right in two lines at east end of the Temple

After this book went to press, the following new registrations
were received from the Museum of Archaeology and Anthropology,
Cambridge, for Appendix D.

MAR, p. 147-155
Add these objects to the distribution list:

1898.26	Flint	
1898.50	Pottery cylinder jar	
1898.79	Pottery bread mould	
1898.82	Pottery necked ovoid jar	143
1898.95	Pottery bowl	
1898.107	Pottery bowl	
1898.229	Limestone mace-head	453
1898.235	Flint	(235)
1898.235a	Flint	(235)
1898.236	Flint	136
1898.237	Flint blade	(237)
1898.238	Flint	(238)
1898.239	Flint blade	(239)
1898.240	Flint	(240)
1898.241	Flint	(241)
1898.242	Flint	(242)
1898.243	Flint	240
1898.244	Flint	(244)
1898.245	Flint	(245)
1898.246	Flint	247
1898.247	Flint	(247)
1898.248	Flint blade	
1898.249	Flint blade	293
1898.250	Flint blade	402
1898.251	Flint	541.0
1898.252	Flint	
1898.253	Flint	
1898.254	Flint	
1898.255	Flint	
1898.256	Flint	284
1898.257-8	Flint	

1898.259	Flint blade	280
1898.260	Flint	
1898.262	Flint	
1898.263	Flint	293
1898.264	Flint	
1898.265	Flint	
1898.266	Flint	
1898.267	Flint	
1898.268	Flint	
1898.269	Flint	282
1898.270	Flint	237
1898.271	Flint	(271)
1898.272	Flint	513
1898.273	Flint	513
1898.273a	Flint	541
1898.275	Slate palette	? 18
1898.278A	Pebble	
1898.278C	Brown pebble	
1898.520	Flint grinder	537
1898.521	Flint	
1898.522	Flint	521, 580
1898.523	Flint	
1898.524	Limestone jar	534
1898.530	Pottery dish	
1898.536	Pottery flaring beaker	
1898.539	Pottery cup	
1898.544	Pottery beaker	
1898.554	Calcite cylinder jar	
1898.560	Calcite cylinder jar	
1898.563	Calcite dish	
1898.564	Calcite dish	453.89
1898.565	Calcite bowl	471
1898.566	Calcite bowl	
1898.567	Calcite dish	471.115
1898.568	Calcite bowl	
1898.569	Pottery lid	

1898.570	Calcite dish	
1898.571	Calcite bowl	471.15a
1898.572	Diorite palette fragment	
1898.574	Calcite bowl	471.114
1898.581	Pottery bowl	
1898.591	Calcite jar	471.5
D1898.50	Pottery cylinder jar	
D1898.51	Pottery cylinder jar	92
D1898.54	Pottery cylinder jar	106
D1898.55	Pottery cylinder jar	
D1898.57	Pottery cylinder jar, W ware	141
D1898.79	Pottery bread mould	
D1898.81	Pottery jar	
D1898.82	Pottery ovoid necked jar	
D1898.86	Pottery necked globular jar	
D1898.89	Pottery "nw" pot	
D1898.93	Calcite dish	471
D1898.95	Pottery bowl	
D1898.105	Pottery dish	
D1898.106	Pottery conical jar lid	
D1898.107	Pottery bowl	
D1898.112	Rectangular slate palette	2
D1898.115	Pottery cylinder jar	
D1898.188	Pottery "nw" pot	
Z1154	Faience necklance	
Z1157	Calcite hippopotamus amulet	
Z16742A	Pottery wavy-handled jar	525
Z16787A	Pottery bowl	520
Z16792	Pottery bowl	
Z16798B	Pottery open vessel	536
Z16799C	Pottery bottle	523
Z16799D	Pottery necked vase	523 D
Z16878	Pottery wavy-handled jar	
Z17187	Flint swallow-tailed knife	
Z38288	Flint	1
Z38291.1-3	Flints	21

Z38293	Flint	60
Z38295.1-5	Flints	
Z38296	Flint	64
Z38298	Flint	72
Z38299	Flint	81
Z38300	Flint	82
Z38302	Flint	88
Z38303.1-6	Flints	86
Z38304	Flint	87
Z38305.1-36	Flints	88
Z38306	Flint	89
Z38307	Flint	
Z38308	Flint	98
Z38309	Flint	99
Z38310	Flint	108
Z38311.1-3	Flints	109
Z38312	Flint	110
Z38313	Flint	120
Z38314	Flint	122
Z38315	Flint	123
Z38316.1-12	Flints	124
Z38317	Flint	125
Z38318.1-3	Flints	126
Z38319	Flint	128
Z38320	Flint	133
Z38321	Flint	135
Z38322	Flint	138
Z38323	Flint	140
Z38324	Flint	144
Z38325	Flint	145
Z38326	Flint	146
Z38327.1-9	Flint	147
Z38328	Flint	148
Z38329	Flint	150
Z38330	Flint	153
Z38331.1-3	Flints	160

Z38332.1-7	Flints	161
Z38333.1-5	Flints	163
Z38334	Flint	164
Z38335	Flint	168
Z38336.1-6	Flints	169
Z38337	Flint	170
Z38338	Flint	172
Z38339	Flint	173
Z38340	Flint	176
Z38341.1-2	Flints	178
Z38342	Flint	180
Z38343	Flint	186
Z38344	Flint	198
Z38345	Flint	199
Z38346	Flint	205
Z38347.1-2	Flints	208
Z38348	Flint	209
Z38349	Flint	210
Z38350	Flint	211
Z38351	Flint	215
Z38352	Flint	221
Z38353	Flint	225
Z38354	Flint	251
Z38355	Flint	500
Z38356	Flint	520
Z38357	Flint	524
Z38358.1-2	Flints	525
Z38359	Flint	526
Z38360	Flint	527
Z38361	Flint	564
Z38362	Flint	577
Z38363	Large flint tool	166
Z38364	Flint	
Z38365.1-5	Flints	
Z38366	Flint	
Z38367	Flint	

Z38368	Flint	
Z38369	Flint	
Z38371	Flint	
Z38372	Copper harpoon	88
Z38373.1-5	Denticulated flint blade with sickle gloss	
Z38373.6-7	Denticulated flint blade	
Z38373.37-47	Flints	
Z38373.48-49	Flint scrapers	
Z38373.50	Red flint flake	
Z38373.51	Flint knife fragment	
Z38373.52	Flint squared blade	
Z38373.53	Flint knife	
Z38373.55	Bifacially worked flint flake	
Z38373.56	Flint half-moon flake	
Z38373.57	White flint pointed tool	
Z38374	Flint	H.ph
Z38375	Flint	1005
Z38376	Flint	1002
Z38377	Flint	?1004
Z38378	Flint	?80
Z38379	Flint	?203
Z38380	Flint	?100
Z38381.1-7	Flints	
Z38386	Flint	
Z38389	Flint	9
Z38390	Flint core	520 3
?Z38391	Flint	18
Z38392	Flint knife	36
Z38394	Flint	62
Z38397	Flint	65
Z38480	Flint axe	502
Z38529	Grinding stone	
Z45134A-E	Flint	10
Z45647	Fragment pottery bread mould	
Z45752	Calcite cylinder jar fragment	

Z45818	Pottery vase, undulating mouth	
Z45820	Pottery model jar, tapering	
Z45823	Basalt bowl fragment	
Z45824	Diorite bowl fragment	
Z45825	Diorite bowl fragment	
Z45826	Pottery sherd	
Z45846	Pottery sherd	
Z45851	Pottery cup	
Z45852	Pottery bowl	
Z45853	Pottery bowl sherd	
Z46991	Clay sealing	168
Z46992	Clay sealing	168

MAR, p. 155-159:

Faculty of Oriental Studies, Cambridge

Two sealings registered as LE 1 - 214 have been transferred to the
Museum of Archaeology and Anthropology, Cambridge, as Z45298-
46137.

BIBLIOGRAPHY

Abbreviations

ARCE   American Research Center in Egypt

ASAE   Annales du Service

BMMA   Bulletin of the Metropolitan Museum of Art

BSAE   British School of Archaeology in Egypt

EES   Egypt Exploration Society

ERA   Egyptian Research Account

GM   Göttinger Miszellen

IFAO   Institut Francais d'Archéologie Orientale du Caire

JARCE   Journal of the American Research Center in Egypt

JEA   Journal of Egyptian Archaeology

JNES   Journal of Near Eastern Studies

JSSEA   Journal of the Society of the Study of Egyptian
            Antiquities

MDAIK   Mitteilungen des Deutschen Archäologischen Instituts
            Abteilung Kairo

Adams   1974   Adams, B., *Ancient Hierakonpolis*, and
                   1974b   *Supplement*, Aris & Phillips, Warminster
                             1974.

Adams   1975   Adams, B., "Petrie's Manuscript Notes on
                             the Koptos foundation deposits of
                             Tuthmosis III", *JEA* 61 (1975), pp.102-111
                             (includes list of Petrie MSS).

Adams   1977   Adams, B., "Hierakonpolis", *Lexicon der
                             Ägyptologie*, Band II, Lieferung 16 (1977),
                             pp.1182-6.

Adams   1982   Adams, B., "Artifacts" (from Locality 6),
                             in Hoffman *et al*, *The Predynastic of
                             Hierakonpolis*, Egyptian Studies Association
                             publication no. 1, Cairo 1982, pp.56-58.

Adams &   1984   Adams, B. & Jaeschke, R., *The Koptos Lions*,
Jaeschke   Contributions in Anthropology and History,
                             no. 3, 1984, Milwaukee Public Museum.

Arens   1984   Arens, W., "The Demise of Kings and the
                             Meaning of Kingship: Royal Funerary
                             Ceremony in the Contemporary Southern
                             Sudan and Renaissance France", *Anthropos*
                             79 (1984), pp.355-367.

Baumgartel   1970   Baumgartel, E., *Petrie's Naqada Excavations:
                             A Supplement*, Quaritch, London 1970.

Bourriau   1984   Bourriau, J., "Egyptian Antiquities
                             Acquired in 1982 by Museums in the United
                             Kingdom", *JEA* 70 (1984), pp.130-135.

Case & Payne   1962   Case, H. & Payne, J.C., "Tomb 100: the
                             decorated tomb at Hierakonpolis", *JEA* 48
                             (1962), pp.9-18.

Castillos   1979   Castillos, J.J., "An Analysis of the Tombs
                             in the Predynastic Cemeteries at Naqada",
                             JSSEA X (1979), pp.21-38.

Castillos   1982   Castillos, J.J., "Analyses of Egyptian
                             Predynastic and Early Dynastic Cemeteries:
                             final conclusions", *JSSEA* XII (1982),
                             pp.29-53.

Castillos   1983   Castillos, J.J., *A Study of the Spatial
                             Distribution of large and richly endowed
                             tombs in Egyptian Predynastic and Early
                             Dynastic Cemeteries*, Toronto 1983.

Downes   1974   Downes (nee Slow), D., *The Excavations at
                            Esna, 1905-6*, Aris & Phillips, Warminster
                            1974.

Drower   1985   Drower, M.S., *Flinders Petrie: a Life in
                            Archaeology*, Gollancz, London 1985.

Fairservis   1971-2   Fairservis, W.A., "Preliminary Report on
                            the first two seasons at Hierakonpolis",
                            JARCE IX (1971-2), pt.1, pp.7-27; pt.V,
                            pp.67-68, figs.1-50.

Fairservis   1983   Fairservis, W.A., *The Hierakonpolis Project:
                            Excavation on the Kom el Gemuwia, Season
                            of 1978*, Occasional Papers in Anthropology,
                            no. I, Vassar College, Poughkeepsie, 1983.

Fairservis   1986   Fairservis, W.A., *The Hierakonpolis Project:
                            excavation of the Archaic remains of the
                            niched gate, Season of 1981*, Occasional
                            Papers in Anthropology, no. III, Vassar
                            College, Poughkeepsie, 1986.

Garstang   1907   Garstang, J., "Excavations at Hierakonpolis"
                            ASAE VIII (1907), pp.136-7, pls.V-VII.

Geller   1984   Geller, J., M.A. thesis: *The Predynastic
                            Ceramics Industry at Hierakonpolis*,
                            Washington University, St. Louis, 1984.

Harlan   1985   Harlan, J.F., Ph.D. thesis: *Predynastic
                            Settlement Patterns: a view from Hierakon-
                            polis*, Washington University, St. Louis,
                            1985.

Hassan   1980   Hassan, F.A., "Prehistoric Settlements
                            along the main Nile", in M.A.J. Williams
                            & H. Faure (eds.), *The Sahara and the Nile*,
                            1980.

Hassan   1981   Hassan, F.A., *Demographic Archaeology*,
                            Academic Press, New York 1981.

Hassan   1984   Hassan, F.A., "Radiocarbon Chronology of
                            Predynastic Naqada Settlements", *Current
                            Anthropology* 25 (1984), pp.681-3.

Hendrickx   1984   Hendrickx, S., "The Late Predynastic
                            Cemetery at El Kab", in L. Krzyzaniak & M.
                            Kobusiewicz (eds.), *Origin and Early
                            Development of Food Producing Cultures in
                            North East Africa*, Poznan 1984, pp.225-230.

| Hoffman | 1971-2 | Hoffman, M.A., "Preliminary Report on the first two seasons at Hierakonpolis", *JARCE* IX (1971-2), pt.III, pp.35-47; pt.IV, pp. 49-66, figs. 1-13, 15-23. |

Hoffman | 1974 | Hoffman, M.A., "The Social Context of Trash Disposal in an Early Dynastic Egyptian Town", *American Antiquity* 39 (1974), pp.35-50.

Hoffman | 1979 | Hoffman, M.A., *Egypt before the Pharaohs,* A.A. Knopf, New York 1979.

Hoffman | 1980a | Hoffman, M.A., "Ghosts in the Sand", *Arts om Virginia Magazine,* Virginia Museum of Fine Arts, 21 (1980), pp.2-17.

Hoffman | 1980b | Hoffman, M.A., "A Rectangular Amratian House from Hierakonpolis and its significance for Predynastic research", *JNES* 39 (1980), pp.119-137.

Hoffman et al | 1982 | Hoffman, M.A. *et al, The Predynastic of Hierakonpolis,* Egyptian Studies Association Publication no. 1, Cairo and Illinois 1982.

Hoffman | 1983 | Hoffman, M.A., "Where Nations Began", *Science 83,* vol.4, no.8 (1983), pp.42-51.

Hoffman | 1986 | Hoffman, M.A., "A Preliminary Report on the 1984 Excavations at Hierakonpolis", *ARCE Newsletter* 131 (1986), pp.3-14.

Hoffman, Hamroush & Allen | forthcoming | Hoffman, M.A., Hamroush, H.A. & Allen, R.O., "The Origins of Urbanism in Ancient Egypt - an interdisciplinary approach", submitted to *American Scientist.*

Hope | 1986 | Hope, C.A., "Egyptian Antiquities in the History Teaching Collection at MacQuarie University", *GM* 90 (1986), pp.87-94.

Kaiser | 1957 | Kaiser, W., "Zur Inneren Chronologie der Naqadakultur", *Archaeologia Geographica* 61 (1957), pp.67-77.

Kaiser & Dreyer | 1982 | Kaiser, W. & Dreyer, G., "Umm el-Qaab: Nachuntersuchungen im frühzeitlichen Königsfriedhof, 2. Vobericht", *MDAIK,* Band 38 (1982), pp.211-269, pls.52-58.

Kemp | 1963 | Kemp, B.J., "Excavations at Hierakonpolis Fort, 1905: a preliminary note", *JEA* 49 (1963), pp.24-28, pls.IV-V.

Kemp   1968   Kemp, B.J., "The Osiris Temple at Abydos",
                             MDAIK (1968), pp.138-155, pls.XXXIX-XLII.

Kemp   1973   Kemp, B.J., "Photographs of the Decorated
                             Tomb at Hierakonpolis", *JEA* 59 (1973),
                             pp.36-43, pls.XXIII-XXV.

Kemp   1977   Kemp, B.J., "The early development of
                             towns in Egypt", *Antiquity* LI (1977),
                             pp.185-200.

Kroeper   1985   Kroeper, K., "Decorated Ware from Minshat
                             Abu Omar", (Munich East Delta Expedition),
                             *Bulletin de Liaison du Groupe Internation-
                             al d'Étude de la Ceramique Égyptienne* X,
                             IFAO (1985), pp.12-17, figs. 1-7.

Lansing   1935   Lansing, A., "The Museum's Excavation at
                             Hierakonpolis", Supplement to the *BMMA*,
                             pt. ii (1935), pp.37-45, 4 figs.

Lupton   1981   Lupton, C., "In Search of the First
                             Pharaohs", *LORE*, vol. 31, no. 3 (1981),
                             pp.3-21.

Lythgoe   1965   Lythgoe, A.M. (ed. Dunham, Dows), *The
                             Predynastic Cemetery N7000: Nag-ed-Dêr*,
                             University of California Publications,
                             Egyptian Archaeology no. 7, 1965.

Metcalf &   1979   Metcalf, P. & Huntingdom, W.R.,
  Huntingdon   *Celebrations of Death*, C.U.P., New York
                             1979.

de Morgan   1909   de Morgan, H., "Étude sur l'Égypte
                             Primitive", *Revue de l'École d'Anthropologie*
                             19 (1909), pt. I, pp.128-140; pt. II, pp.
                             263-281

de Morgan   1912   de Morgan, H., "Report on excavations made
                             in Upper Egypt during the winter 1907-1908",
                             ASAE 12 (1912), pp.22-50.

Needler   1981   Needler, W., "Federn's Revision of Petrie's
                             Predynastic Pottery Classification", *JSSEA*
                             XI (1981), pp.69-74.

Needler   1984   Needler, W., *Predynastic and Archaic Egypt
                             in the Brooklyn Museum*, The Brooklyn
                             Museum, New York 1984.

Payne   1973   Payne, J.C., "The Decorated Tomb at Hiera-
                             konpolis Confirmed", *JEA* 59 (1973), pp.
                             31-35.

Petrie	1921	Petrie, W.M.F., *Corpus of Prehistoric Pottery and Palettes*, BSAE, 1921.
Petrie	1953	Petrie, W.M.F., *Corpus of Protodynastic Pottery*, BSAE, 1953.
Petrie & Quibell	1896	Petrie, W.M.F. & Quibell, J.E., *Naqada and Ballas*, ERA, 1896.
Quibell	1900	Quibell, J.E., *Hierakonpolis* I, ERA, 1900.
Quibell & Green	1902	Quibell, J.E. & Green, F.W., *Hierakonpolis* II, ERA, 1902.
Reisner	1936	Reisner, G.A., *The Development of the Egyptian Tomb down to the Accession of Cheops*, Harvard University Press, Massachusetts, 1936.
Saad	1945-7	Saad, Z.Y., *The Royal Excavations at Helwan*, Cairo 1945-7.
Saad	1969	Saad, Z.Y., *The Excavations at Helwan*, University of Oklahoma Press, 1969.
Saxe	1970	Saxe, A.A., Ph.D. thesis: *Social Dimensions of Mortuary Practice*, University of Michigan, Ann Arbor, 1970.
Slow	1963-4	Slow, D., "An Ivory Fragment from Hierakonpolis, Upper Egypt", *Liverpool Bulletin* (1963-4), pp.13-18, pls.1-4.
Spencer	1980	Spencer, A.J., *Catalogue of Egyptian Antiquities in the British Museum V: Early Dynastic Objects*, London 1980.
Vermeersch	1978	Vermeersch, P.M., *El Kab II: L'El Kabien, Épipalaeolithic de la Vallee du Nil Égyptien*, Publications du Comite des Fouilles Belges en Égypte, Leuven 1978.
Wildung	1984	Wildung, D., "Terminal Prehistory of the Nile Delta, Theses" in L. Krzyzaniak & M. Kobusiewicz (eds.), *Origin and Early Development of Food Producing Cultures in North East Africa*, Poznan 1984, pp.265-269.

<u>PLATES</u>

GRAVES INCLUDED WITH NEGATIVE NUMBERS (see Appendix B)

Grave 6 (H1)	Grave 66 (H96)
Grave 8 (H3)	Grave 68 (H51)
Grave 9 (H4)	Grave 70 (H54)
Grave 10 (H6)	Grave 71 (H55)
Grave 11 (H8)	Grave 74 (H58)
Grave 16 (H11)	Grave 76 (H59)
Graves 19-20 (H16)	Grave 81 (H61)
Grave 25 (H23)	Grave 88 (H64)
Grave 26 (H24)	Graves 88-89 (H65)
Grave 28 (H26)	Grave 90 (H66)
Grave 29 (H28)	Grave 92 (H70)
Grave 32 (H30)	Grave 94 (H22)
Grave 35 (H33)	Grave 95 (H71)
Grave 37 (H36)	Grave 96 (H72)
Grave 42 (H37)	Grave 97 (H73)
Grave 43 (H38)	Grave 101 (H74)
Grave 47 (H39)	Grave 107 (H76)
Grave 50 (H42)	Grave 108 (H95)
Grave 51 (H45)	Graves 110-111 (H78)
Grave 53 (H44)	Grave 140 (H79)
Grave 56 (H86)	Grave 141 (H82)
Grave 60 (H46)	Grave 142 (H83)
Grave 61 (H49)	Graves near south wall, west of gate (H108)
Grave 62 (H47)	

Grave 8 (H3)

Grave 6 (H1)

PLATE 1

Grave 10 (H6)

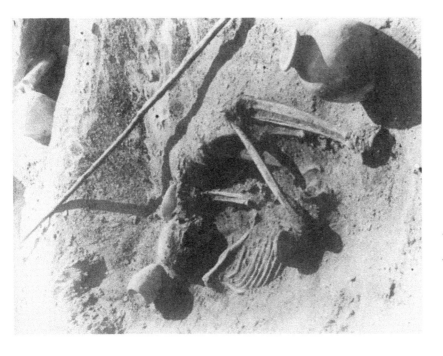

Grave 9 (H4)

PLATE 2

Grave 16 (H11)

Grave 11 (H8)

PLATE 3

Grave 25 (H23)

Grave 19-20 (H16)

PLATE 4

Grave 28 (H26)

Grave 26 (H24)

PLATE 5

Grave 29 (H28)

Grave 32 (H30)

PLATE 6

Grave 37 (H36)

Grave 35 (H33)

PLATE 7

PLATES

Reproduction of all photographs courtesy of School of Archaeology and Oriental Studies, University of Liverpool.

Grave 42 (H37)

Grave 43 (H38)

PLATE 8

Grave 47 (H39)

Grave 50 (H42)

PLATE 9

Grave 53 (H44)

Grave 51 (H45)

PLATE 10

Grave 56 (H86)
This also shows a brick structure
in the centre of the Fort

Grave 60 (H46)

PLATE 11

Grave 62 (H47)

Grave 61 (H49)

PLATE 12

Grave 66 (H96)

Grave 68 (H51)

PLATE 13

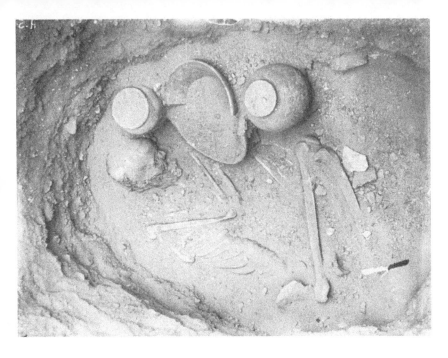

Grave 71 (H55)

Grave 70 (H54)

PLATE 14

Grave 74 (H58)

Grave 76 (H59)

PLATE 15

Grave 81 (H61)

Grave 88 (H64)

PLATE 16

Graves 88-89 (H65)
This also shows a brick structure in the centre
of the Fort.

Grave 90 (H66)

PLATE 17

Grave 93 (H70)

Grave 92 (H69)

PLATE 18

Grave 94 (H22)

Grave 95 (H71)

PLATE 19

Grave 96 (H72)

Grave 97 (H73)

PLATE 20

Grave 101 (H74)

Grave 107 (H76)

PLATE 21

Grave 108 (H95)

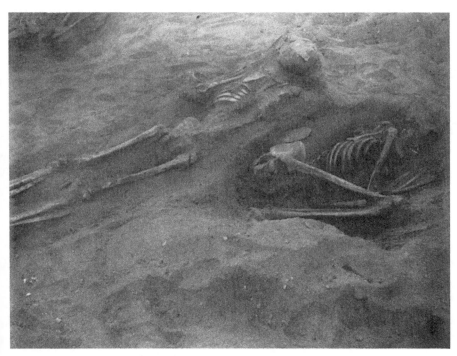

Grave 110-111 (H78)

PLATE 22

Grave 140 (H79)

Grave 141 (H82)

PLATE 23

Grave 142 (H83)

Graves near south wall, west of Fort gate (H108)
This also shows Harold Jones

PLATE 24

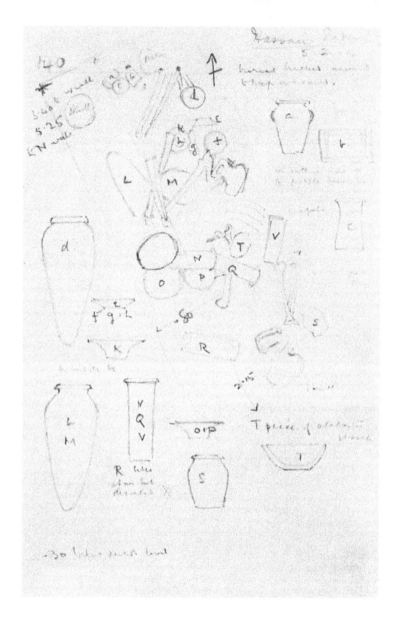

PLATE 25

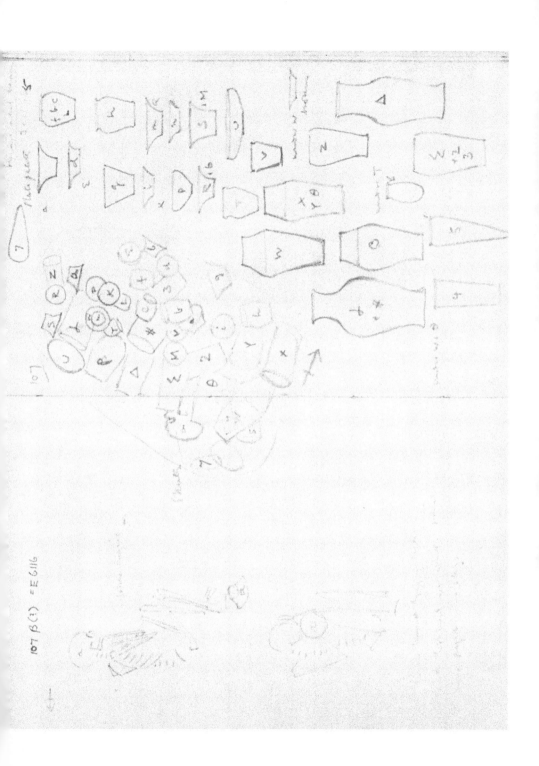

PLATE 26

PLAN OF FORT CEMETERY (ENDPIECE)

Graves on Garstang's MS Map	Graves Plotted by Kemp				Graves Plotted by Adams
6	18	78	110	147B	37
7	19	79	111	148	38
8	20	80	112	149	39
9	42	81	113	150	45
10	43	82	114	151	58
11	44	83	115	153	67
12	46	84	116	154	
13	47	85	117	155	
14	48	86	118	156	
15	49	87	119	157	
15A	51	88	122	158	
16	52	89	123	159	
17	53	89A	124	160	
21	54	90	125	161	
22	56	91	126	163	
23	57	92	128	164	
24	60	93	129	165	
25	61	94	130	166	
26	62	95	131	167	
28	63	96	132	168	
30	64	97	133	169	
31	66	98	134	170	
32	68	99	136	171	
33	69	100	137	172	
34	70	101	138		
35	71	102	139		
36	72	103	140		
	73	105	141		
	74	106	142		
	75	107	145		
	76	108	146		
	77	109	147		

9 780415 865265